Reflections of a Secular Franciscan

I0159225

A LAYPERSON'S GUIDE TO
THE SECULAR FRANCISCAN
WAY OF LIFE

Writings by
Ruth Vogel, S.F.O.

As a Candidate,
Professed Member
and Formation Director
of the
Secular Franciscan Order

Table of Contents

Introduction

I The Secular Franciscan Order

II Reflections on St. Francis and His Early Companions

III The Franciscan Way of Life

About the cover: The Tau cross shown on the cover of this book was drawn by St. Francis on a blessing document he gave Brother Leo. (See page 87).

Ruth Vogel, S.F.O.
January 21, 1910 - May 26, 1998

About Ruth Vogel, S.F.O.

January 21, 1910 – May 26, 1998

Ruth was born in Columbus Ohio, one of four sisters. When she was about 10 years of age she and her family moved to Virginia. As a young woman she worked as a secretary for the Army/Navy Register, but had to retire early on disability because of poor vision.

She lived with her sister Leona for a time in Arlington Virginia, neither girl was married. She was professed a member of the Secular Franciscan Order on January 8th, 1967 at Sacred Heart Fraternity in Arlington. Some time later she and Leona, "the girls" as the rest of the family called them, packed up their belongings and assorted dogs and cats in their Volkswagen and moved to Florida.

Ruth became a member of the "Little Flowers of St. Francis Fraternity," which was then called "St. Brendan's Fraternity" at St. Brendan's Church in Ormond Beach, Florida and was a member there for many years (her trip to Assisi was a most memorable time in her life, as documented in her journal.) Her greatest contribution to her fraternity and the Franciscan Order was her devotion and inspiration as formation director.

Ruth wrote many articles and poems for her fraternity, the "Franciscan Herald" and other Franciscan publications. Her love for Jesus and her saintly devotion to the Blessed Mother and St. Francis was full of humility and pious fervor. She not only had the gift of perception in the Franciscan way of life, but also the ability to enter into the middle of Francis' thoughts, whether it was describing the wonders of God's creation or Franciscan spirituality.

Her ability to put into words a scene which she would describe, whether it was the life of St. Francis or showing the "Way of St. Francis" to those who were candidates or professed members, was inspiring.

The reader should not hurry through her words, but meditate and savor the feeling and emotion she had when she described a scene or explained Franciscan spirituality. We are sure you will find her writings an inspiration and a joy to read.

Ruth put volumes of her thoughts on paper, some typed and some hand written, which I had the privilege to edit and compile in this first book. It is the intention of the "Little Flowers of St. Francis Fraternity" and the "Five Franciscan Martyrs Region" to make her writings available to everyone, whether they are candidates, professed members, or anyone who would like to have a closer relationship with our Lord.

A few of her words sum up our reason for wanting to bring this book to you:

"I have always had a great love for God and for the Blessed Virgin, even when I was a little girl. I believed in them without question. But, for so many years, this was a superficial feeling in my life — until I was exposed to the "Franciscan Way." Then from the very beginning, when I found Francis, it suddenly burgeoned on me — my faith became intense, vibrant and alive. This Jesus was no longer casual; my God was no longer a vague being somewhere out there in the stratosphere. He was around me, in me, alive in my life, living right in my house with me.

"I could go on and on talking about what this great compassionate friend Francis is to me now. Why would I ever need to turn elsewhere to find my Jesus and my God? This is the charisma of St. Francis. How can I make other people see it -- Feel it?" ..."As Secular Franciscans, we are committed to be Christ's hands, mouth, feet, HIMSELF, in the world. We are to be His heralds and workers, using our talents, opportunities, words, and actions to communicate His message, so that He walks and talks and comes to life through us, for all people."

I would like to thank the members of the Little Flowers Fraternity, the Rev. Thomas K. Murphy, O.F.M., Regional Spiritual Assistant; Deacon Richard Nagle, S.F.O., and Pamela Nagle, S.F.O., for their support. I would like to mention also, my wife, Marge, and Pam Nagle, SFO who helped with the editing of the articles; my sons, Mike, who helped with the design the cover and Greg who helped with the format of the book.

I must say though, that when I had a problem or needed help, Ruth, was always there spiritually to solve the problem, make a point or find something I needed. She was uncanny and definitely in the middle of this whole project. God bless her. I hope she had as much Franciscan joy as I did.

Dennis R. Mallon, S.F.O.,

Little Flowers of St. Francis Fraternity

On Feburary 22, 1998, Ruth Vogel, S.F.O. addressed a letter of permission to publish her writings to Pamela Nagle, S.F.O. and Deacon Richard Nagle, S.F.O., Regional Executive Council members of the Five Franciscan Martyrs Region, Secular Franciscan Order.

Edited by Dennis R. Mallon, S.F.O., with editing assistance by Pamela Nagle, S.F.O.

All references to Holy Scripture are from "Good News for Modern Man," Third Edition.

I preach constantly and sometimes I speak words.

Words attributed to St. Francis of Assisi

There was a Boy

A little poem on the successful
formation of a beloved and well-known Saint.

There was a boy, a quite willful,
show-off, teen-aged brat;
Who wakened folks at midnight,
With loud singing and all that.

Who spent his father's money
As though it were going out of style;
But, who suddenly had a vision
And then in a very little while —

Became so hooked on Jesus
He was never again the same.
He reached the heights of sainthood,
And came alive in Jesus' name!

We're speaking of St. Francis,
Believe it if you can!
Our noisy, willful laddy boy
Became that saintly man.

So, Secular Franciscans,
It's so very plain to see
That what happened to our Francis,
Proves there's hope for you and me.

Ruth Vogel, S.F.O.

I The Secular Franciscan Order

A Brief History of the
Third Order of St. Francis

When Francis founded his Order of Penance for people living in the world in the early 13th century, the idea was not original with him. There were other movements of a like nature before that. However, he did start the Order of Penance, or Third Order of St. Francis as it came to be known, in 1209.

In that year, after St. Francis received the oral approval of Pope Innocent III for his "Lesser Brothers," he went about preaching the Kingdom of God. He amazed people with his zeal. With astonishment they listened to him. "Isn't he that playboy of Assisi, son of Peter Bernadone?" they asked. Doesn't that remind us of Jesus when the people asked in amazement, *"Isn't this the son of Joseph, the carpenter and of Mary?* Many were drawn to Francis by his magnetic sincerity and love of God.

Thomas of Celano said Francis "mapped out for them a way of salvation in their various stations of life."

In 1221 Pope Honorius III ordered the Bishop of Rimini to take the Brothers of Penance at Faenza under his protection. They were being pushed around by civil authorities because they were refusing to take the oath of military service, saying it was forbidden under their rule. The mayor had been trying to force them to take the oath which would have obliged them to take up arms whenever the whims of the authorities ordered it.

Also, in the same year 1221, Cardinal Ugolino took the original short rule of 1209 and put it in legal writing, and Pope Honorius III approved it.

Most authors have regarded St. Francis' "Letter to All the Faithful" as the most original form of the rule of the Third Order. This letter is produced in full in the "St. Francis of Assisi: Early Documents."

The rule just mentioned of Cardinal Ugolino (later to become Pope Gregory IX) contains some regulations with which we are very familiar and which affect us now.

1. Attendance at monthly meetings.
2. A list of officers a fraternity should have.
3. External means of attaining holiness, such as poverty and simplicity of living.

4. Internal means of attaining holiness: prayer; Sacraments of penance and Holy Communion; nightly examination of conscience and hearing the word of God.

5. They had an office — the Divine Office if they could read (which few of them could) or 54 Paters, Aves and Glorias for those who could not read.

6. Prayer for the living and deceased members.

7. Special charities (Apostolates).

8. Provide a common fund for the needs of the fraternity and others who are in need.

They were not allowed to take oaths and so could not hold public office. And they were to observe strict rules of fasting. These latter two rules have been greatly modified.

In 1289 Cardinal Ugolino's rule was supplanted by that of Nicholas IV. This new rule gave to all fraternities a uniform charter. It changed the rule about bearing arms to allow it for defense of the Church, the Faith of Christ, and one's country.

Among the first secular Franciscans were Blessed Luchesio Modestini of Poggibonzi and his wife, Buonadonna.

Factually, Francis did not give a rule to Luchesio and Buonadonna until 1218. The Third Order had been in existence for 9 years at that time.

Some other known "firsts" are: A lawyer, Bartholomew of Romagna and the Roman patrician, Matthew Orsini, father of Pope Nicholas III.

Well known to us from our readings is Count Orlando of Cattanii, who had given Francis the beautiful mountain of La Verna where he received the stigmata and Blessed John Velita whom we know as the "Holy John." Thomas of Celano mentions John as the one whom Francis sent for to set up the first manger scene at Greccio.

And, not to be outshone by the men, there are renowned female secular Franciscans: The Lady Giacoma of Settesoli, a Roman lady of noble birth whom Francis called Brother Jacopa and Blessed Veridiana. Veridiana became a recluse in 1208 at the age of 26 and had herself walled up in a cell next to a chapel in Florence and spent the remaining 34 years of her life there in prayer and penance. In 1222 St. Francis visited her and gave her the habit. There is also Queen Elizabeth of Hungary, who became the patroness of the Third Order and her kinswoman, Queen Elizabeth of Portugal.

Pope Leo XIII, when he was Archbishop of Perugia in 1871, and on the occasion of the golden jubilee of Pius IX as a secular, wrote a pastoral letter on the Third Order. The following year he, himself, joined the Third Order in the Franciscan Friary of Honte Ripido near Perugia.

During the centuries following Nicholas IV's rule many changes had taken place by papal decree. Pope Leo, in 1883, revised the old rule of Nicholas IV, adapting it to his times and conditions but kept its nature, character, and spirit intact.

The long habit had been changed to a large scapular and cord, which was worn on the outside. Later this became a small scapular and cord, which were worn on the inside.

Pope Leo XIII pointed out that the rigorous rule of Nicholas IV was not suited to modern times and customs, which limited the Third Order to a small number of people.

Hence, he modernized the rule and opened the Third Order to all good Catholics who were earnest about striving for Christian perfection. The first two Orders, he said, are for those favored by God with the grace of a rare zeal, while the Third Order was to accommodate many.

The rule was again revised to suit the late twentieth century needs, but again the nature and spirit have been kept intact.

This present Rule for the Secular Franciscan Order was approved by Pope Paul VI, June 24, 1978. It is known as the Pauline Rule.

At least 53 members of the Third Order of St. Francis have been canonized and [about] 76 have been beatified.

Some Basic Requirements of the Secular Franciscan Order

1. Knowledge of St. Francis
2. Apostolic Life of St. Francis
3. Nature and Purpose of the Order
4. Community Life
5. Spirit of St. Francis

1. Knowledge of St. Francis

It is not enough to know a factual history of St. Francis' life — not just what he said and did; but more importantly, what he felt and believed in. It is a probing into his inner most thoughts, his struggles, motivations and his SPIRIT — not just the what and the when, but the WHY.

Reading is all-important, like biographies, but not just one and not just bits and snatches of any one, but the whole book.

Scripture reading is important. Not just reading, either; but, pondering and assimilating the MESSAGE; listening to the over-all message and using the little messages in one's daily living.

2. Apostolic Life of St. Francis

The First Order, the Friars Minor, Observants, Capuchins and Conventuals are members who were required by Francis to give all their goods to the poor, to pray intensely, serve lepers and the poor, and to live in peace and brotherly love and service to all.

The Second Order, known as the Poor Ladies, or Poor Clares, was founded by St. Clare, under St. Francis' Rule and guidance, in 1212. This was a cloistered community of women who lived under the austere poverty advocated by St. Francis, who established them at the little church of San Damiano.

The Third Order founded in 1209 was for lay people who aspired to follow the life and spirit of St. Francis while remaining in the world. Simple frugality of living, prayer, peace and brotherly love were their norm.

Francis' remarkable example, his compassion and universal love for all people and all things created by God, were an outgrowth of his passionate love for Jesus Christ and His Blessed Mother Mary. His concern for the Universe was shown beautifully in his "Canticle of Brother Sun," known also as the "Canticle of the Creatures."

In recent times he has been designated as the patron of ecology.

In 1224, while he fasted and prayed on Mount La Verna he received the sacred Stigmata on his hands, feet, and side. He was a perfect example of patience in suffering, of which he had an abundance in addition to the Stigmata. But, in spite of his physical afflictions, he carried on his apostolate of preaching and serving, even when he was nearly blind and could no longer walk because his feet were crippled by the wounds of the stigmata.

On October 3rd or 4th, 1226, he died at his beloved Portiuncula, the sanctuary he dedicated to Our Lady, the little church he himself rebuilt, Our Lady of the Angels. He made this little church the cradle of his three Orders. It is now enshrined almost like a little doll's house inside the great basilica of St. Mary of the Angels just outside Assisi. Two years after his death he was canonized.

3. Nature and Purpose of the Order

The unity of the Church, from the time of the apostles down through the popes, the bishops, the priests, and the laity, is centered in the See of St. Peter in Rome.

In Rome, the Rule of the Franciscan Order was approved, at first informally, then formally in writing.

Therefore, we who are members of the Order are sent by the Church to further Christ's work on earth. Our Order belongs to the Church and we are committed to be evangelizers.

We are dedicated to strive for Christian perfection as faithful members of the Catholic Church and members of our fraternity. Our way is the way of Gospel living in our secular world, following the message and spirit of St. Francis of Assisi.

Therefore, it is necessary for us to strive to know what that spirit and message is. To supply that information is the point of these instructions.

Francis wrote his first rule directly from the Gospel teachings of Jesus Christ and we are committed to the task of making present the charisma of St. Francis.

The lay followers of Francis were advised by him to dedicate themselves to a life of penance and simple living right in their homes and places of work. Francis brought about renewal in the Church under the rule of his three Orders for priests, religious, and the laity, all of which were approved by the Pope.

We seculars are members of his great Franciscan family in the life and mission of the Church.

The Secular Franciscan Order is a union of fraternities throughout the world, open to all the faithful. Secular Franciscans strive for perfect charity right in their own environment, bringing that charity and evangelization into action in their own life style.

4. Community Life

Jesus said, *"The command that I give you is that you love one another."*

This is the basis upon which we should build our life in the Franciscan community. This community life takes place for each of us in our fraternities.

To achieve brotherly love in fraternity, and elsewhere, requires that we diligently cultivate the virtues of humility, meekness, patience, gentleness, kindness, tolerance, honesty and tactfulness. A peace-loving commitment and concern for the other members of the fraternity should be the endeavor of each member.

St. Francis reached out to everyone as his brother or sister. As a rule, he always had at least one of his brothers as a companion wherever he went.

Secular Franciscans should look upon the other members of their fraternity in this same spirit; one in Christ, one in the spirit of St. Francis, and one in the spirit with each other.

Coming together in a reunion of their community life at least once a month, they should aid one another wherever needs arise. They should also act together in works of charity and apostolates. It is impossible to be a true Franciscan alone.

The Holy Spirit moves in each one of us. Each is imbued with a deep love for Jesus under the paternal blessedness of our Heavenly Father and the Holy Spirit. Thus, a Secular Franciscan should be gentle and courteous, cheerful, and be at the service of all of his or her Franciscan brothers and sisters in the fraternity.

5. Spirit of St. Francis

The most important aid in formation of a Secular Franciscan is the spirit of St. Francis. What is this spirit?

It is to KNOW Jesus as Francis did, the poor Jesus, the humble Jesus. As St. Paul says, *"You are the people of God; he loved you and chose you for his own. So then, you must put on compassion, kindness, humility, gentleness, and patience. Be helpful to one another, and forgive one another, whenever any of you has a complaint against someone else. You must forgive each other in the same way that the Lord has forgiven you. And to all these add love, which binds all things together in perfect unity. (Col. 3: 12-14).*

As we go our Gospel way with Christ at our side, we strive for harmonious relations with our brothers and sisters in the world; with the Church and its teachings; with its liturgies; with the pope, the bishops and the priests.

We are in continual renewal of our *"metanoia,"* (a Greek word meaning *"radical inner conversion").*

fostered by prayer and the Sacraments, particularly the Holy Eucharist.

We imitate Mary, our Mother.

We surrender to the will of the Father.

We imitate Jesus, the poor one — our suffering servant.

Our lifestyle is simple, humble, unostentatious — a striving for purity of heart, with a deep concern for the poor and deprived of the world.

We share our time and energies in the service of others.

We are promoters of justice.

We carry out our part in the continuing creation and redemption that never ends by the work we do — occupational, family, neighborhood, parish and the market place. We should be an example of Christ's love at all times in all places.

We should be respectful of and careful stewards of all of God's creation, animate and inanimate.

And most important, we should be instruments of God's peace.

Questions:

What do you think is the charismatic spirit and message of St. Francis?

How could use your abilities to aid spiritually, mentally, and physically, the other members of your fraternity?

Do you think you would derive aid, spiritual or otherwise, from meeting with the members of the fraternity at the monthly gatherings. Think about this in depth. Ask Jesus to help you be absolutely honest in answering these questions.

Notes

"Read, Think and Pray."

Thoughts about Becoming a Franciscan

What is the Franciscan message for me?

A good Franciscan example is the best teacher of all. It is worth a thousand instructions, a thousand books. It leads and says, "This is the way. Come follow me."

A good prayer life is also essential. Every person must establish his or her own prayer pattern for each day, including, if at all possible, Mass and Communion. A while ago we said that reading was all-important; now we add, we need to pray, pray, pray. And we need to think and meditate — *Read, think and pray.* Pray to the Holy Spirit to help your thoughts zero in on the MESSAGE.

What is the message for me, how can I use it in my daily living?

How can I use it in my ongoing formation?

Francis' conversion was an ongoing process, it didn't happen one bright morning in Assisi. It took years, sometimes agonizing years for him.

When one is professed it is only the beginning. Formation begins on the day a candidate attends the first instruction class, and it ends the day of his or her death.

A Franciscan in formation, which means every one of us, should go about like a lighted candle — simple and humble. The thought comes to me of the sacred Host that is so ordinary to look at; yet so EXTRAORDINARY in the vastness of what it is.

We are Pilgrims on our way — peaceful and quiet.

Remember a lighted candle doesn't make any noise, but everybody knows it is there.

How do Secular Franciscan strive for spiritual perfection?

They do it the Gospel way. They strive to follow the way, the truth, and the life of Jesus and try to come to KNOW Jesus intimately. First of all, they endeavor to bring about an inward radical conversion (metanoia), and they do this by an ongoing stripping away of worldly inclinations and taking on instead, Christ-centeredness. They try to rid themselves of their own absorption with their own ideas, their own egotism, their wanting their own way — then take on an openness to the ways, thoughts, suggestions, etc. of others. It is important for a Secular Franciscan, at all times, to be an example of Gospel-living in the world where he lives.

The S.F.O. can be looked upon as a school of perfection because sincere dedication to following its ways helps to mold us in a pattern that points our steps in a forward direction towards spiritual perfection.

Is the Secular Franciscan Way the best way to salvation?

Not necessarily the best, but a candidate can be absolutely sure that there is no more exalted charisma than that of St. Francis of Assisi. The very fact that it is called the Gospel Way is proof of this truth. The Gospel Way is the way of Jesus Christ. You can't top that. His way Is the perfect way.

Is the S.F.O. a purely devotional society?

No, we are lay People. Our Franciscan life takes place in our neighborhood, in the community, in the marketplace; among people in all walks of life. Our next door neighbor is our concern. Our parish, government, ecology, and all of God's creation are our concern. We live a dual role: First: devotional — our prayer life is absolutely essential to being a good Franciscan. Second: our life in the world — It is very aptly put in our Rule, we go from "Gospel to life and from life to Gospel." One does not end and the other begin; they intermesh, bound together like Siamese twins, one cannot exist without the other.

Is profession in the Secular Franciscan Order a permanent commitment?

Yes. Inquirers about the Secular Franciscan way are persons who have answered a call by God to intensify a striving for holiness by following the Franciscan way. One is not quite satisfied to let things drift as they have been. One has a feeling that there is so much more to the spiritual side of life than they have been experiencing. The question will present itself, "Will I find the answer to my need for a stronger spiritual life in this Franciscan way?" As you attend the regular meetings and open yourselves to instructions, the answer to that question will unfold for you. Either it will be the way for you; or it will not.

Now, in our "Ritual" we have this:

"On behalf of this fraternity, I warmly welcome you, and I note your desire to inquire into the Secular Franciscan way of life. Be assured that in your search you will have the support and the encouragement of our prayer, our formation and our example. And always keep in mind the words of St. Francis to Brother Leo: 'In whatever way you think will best please our Lord God and follow in his footsteps and in poverty, take that way with the Lord God's blessing.'" *(From the Ritual of the Secular Franciscan Order, Ceremony of Introduction and Welcoming,).*

After you go through the ceremony of Reception, you, a candidate, become an active member, and go on preparing yourselves for a *permanent commitment* when you will be professed.

From the beginning of your inquiry, you will be engaged in a gradual step by step process of working towards a life-long commitment to intensify your striving for spiritual perfection.

The entire Fraternity has an obligation to help you to shape yourself in this way by their example.

In this formative period you will be guided into forming yourselves in the Gospel way by using what you have learned in the instruction sessions, and taking them right with you into your every-day living situations. The Franciscan way should begin to live with you.

As you grow in the knowledge of Jesus Christ, He will become a more a intimate part of your life. You will be going from Jesus in the Gospels to Jesus in you. You will be lifting Jesus out of the pages of the Gospel and bring Him to life in your every-day existence. He will begin to live within your conscious, rather than in your subconscious.

You will come to know better this person, Jesus. He will be a live person walking right with you wherever you go.

The formation of a Secular Franciscan is indeed a lengthy process in which each of you, and each of us, individually, form ourselves minute by minute and day by day and year by year.

And so, for you who are new to this way of life, you will gradually come to a voluntarily and purposeful commitment to step across the threshold of a new environment where you will find yourselves happily and permanently part of the way of St. Francis.

Now, I have a question for you: Is the Secular Franciscan Order for me and am I called to live it?

Notes

Notes

" 'Put on Christ.'
It's a full-time occupation. "

What is Franciscanism

Franciscanism is looking into the face of Jesus and saying, like in the song, "Getting to know you; getting to know all about you; getting to love you; getting to hope you love me."

Franciscanism is our conscious and deliberate movement towards Jesus in this our work-a-day world. It is moving towards him to the point where he becomes a part of our morning, our afternoon and our night and our enjoyment in everything we do. Jesus becomes part of us in the sky and the sea; in the trees and the grass and in sunshine, star shine and moonlight. We see him in the rain and know him in the winds and the fragrances of flowers; we find Him in the satisfaction of music and the laughter of people — yes, and in their tears and cries of pain; we feel his presence where a dog is barking and wagging his tail, and where birds are singing and nesting; when a bus load of people go by or an airplane flies overhead and when we come upon foot prints in the sand. It is to know him to the point where we can say to Him, "Jesus, do you smell that coffee and that bacon cooking?" It is where we can say "Jesus" with confidence when we are in pain or our feelings are hurt or in a million other sad and happy things. Jesus, I know you are here — here at home, and in my neighbor's home, and in those ghetto homes, and in the tin shacks of the very poor — yes, and in the mansions of the rich.

I can see you in all these things, Jesus — you, who by choice, was born poor among the poor.

Franciscanism is our awakening, and our growing awareness of, and our closing in on Christ in everything we see, hear or feel and everything we say, think or do.

St. Paul put it simply, *"Put on Christ."* It's a full-time occupation.

". . . professed Secular
Franciscans express what
Christ means to them by the
very structure of their lives. "

Why Be
A Secular Franciscan

What advantage is there in living a professed Gospel way of Life?

Basically, the way of the Commandments of God is the way that leads to perfection. Actually, the way of the Commandments is encompassed in living up to the first two commandments: to love God all out, and to love our neighbor as ourselves. Our challenge as Secular Franciscans is to LIVE these two commandments. Only by LIVING them can we hope to mold ourselves as dedicated Secular Franciscans seeking spiritual perfection in closer union with God.

Professed Secular Franciscans, like the religious, are a visible sign, a witness and an inspiration to all those who they meet. This thought is a great challenge to our responsibility as a Secular Franciscan.

Religious and professed Secular Franciscans express what Christ means to them by the very structure of their lives. All in the Church are called upon to observe the evangelical councils of poverty, chastity and obedience. In a religious and professed Secular Franciscan they become visible and tangible, a Religious taking these vows and a Secular Franciscan professing publicly to live in the spirit of them. By living in the spirit, God becomes real to us and this reality of God in our lives can bring our humanity to the fulfillment that comes from sharing in the Divinity of Christ."

The Gospel life must be lived in such a way that Secular Franciscans witness to it. This is such a very important thing for us to keep in mind at all times. If we do not bear the responsibility we could risk the possibility of becoming a scandal.

To help us live the reality of God in our lives we need faith without questioning. We should help others believe by ourselves praying and living the faith.

People must see from our lives that God exists and that He brings happiness to those who follow in the Gospel footsteps of His Son.

When we radiate joy because of our close association with Christ we help others to believe and experience in themselves, more and more, the spiritual riches available through Christ.

Notes

*"The cornerstone
on which a Secular Franciscan
builds a simple life style is Jesus;
His sense of values
should be ours. "*

The Rule

*"At the time Ruth wrote this article the Secular Franciscan Order was
using the Constitutions of the Secular Franciscan Order of 1959. The editor
has selected, here, some aspects of the Rule that Ruth felt very important.*

*The reader may get a updated version of the current Rule by referring to
the new Constitutions approved by Rome in December 2000 and which came
effective in the United States in March of 2001. "*

Our Rule is to follow Christ as Francis did

Our Franciscan Rule is an updated version of the original Rule of St.
Francis of Assisi. It is an expression of the ideals of St. Francis and his
personal charisma. It is set forth in a practical manner for members of the
Secular Franciscan Order who are living in today's world. It is not a set of
legal prescriptions and a set of "do this," and "do that" and "don't do that"
and "don't do this." It is a way of life, full of ideals, virtues, and self-imposed
disciplines, that follow the leadership of Francis of Assisi. It is the way of
love of Christ as shown to us in the pages of the Gospels.

The Rule is a guide that opens up to the vastness of the Gospel message. It
is a stepping-stone to the Gospels and Gospel ideals, and thence to closer
union with Christ.

The Prologue to the Rule is a very concise version of St. Francis' "Letter
to all the Faithful." This letter has been called the most beautiful of all of
St. Francis' writings.

The Prologue, like that letter to all the faithful, is divided into two parts: an
exhortation and a warning for those who do penance and those who do not do
penance; or those who have a change of heart, and those who do not have a
change of heart.

Those who do penance are those who turn their hearts to Christ as a flower turns to the sunlight. They embrace the principles of Christ. The result is that,

Those who do penance are those who turn their hearts to Christ as a flower turns to the sunlight. They embrace the principles of Christ. The result is that it reaps happiness in mind and heart and they become intimately involved in the divine life of the Father, the Son, and the Holy Spirit. This is a drastic contrast with those who do not do penance and are caught up in our modern day permissive society."

I am sure that we Franciscans are striving valiantly to cultivate this change of heart. We are trying to do what St. Francis taught us — to give kind reception to these fragrant words of our Lord Jesus Christ from the Scriptures, which St. Francis interspersed richly and lavishly throughout his life.

This Rule is following of the way, the truth, the life, and the love of Christ.

The Rule is not an abstract, detached work of art, sitting out in front of us on a pedestal to be admired and gawked at. We are the Rule — it is written on our hearts. To read it thoroughly, we need to look deep inside and say yes once again to living the gospel of Jesus in the spirit of St. Francis according to the needs of the times.

The text shines through our everyday actions. Our commitment has to be made anew in Jesus Christ, to new ways of doing things. Our commitment here is to study the Rule in depth.

Our Rule is to Know Jesus Intimately

It states very definitely that we, as followers of St. Francis, must zero in on the Christ of the Gospels. We must pluck Jesus bodily out of the pages of the Gospels and set Him in motion, alive and dynamic, right where we are at any given moment. We must encounter Him in our work, in our churches, in our homes and in the marketplaces — everywhere.

We must come to know Him as intimately as we know each member of our own family. We must anticipate what His reaction would be in any particular situation we find ourselves. We should ask ourselves, "what would He say?" The answer is: we should let Him influence us in what we say and do.

We must try to be like St. Francis and be occupied with Jesus and like Francis, Jesus must be in every member of our body. Let's pause here and reflect on that.

If Jesus was to suddenly stride through that door nearest you, what would He look like to you? BRING HIM TO LIFE.

To follow Jesus is the Secular Franciscan's "way of Life?" What do we mean by the words, *"way of life?"*

A *"way of life"* is something that is with us all the time, this minute, and every minute of every hour of every day, week, month, year and all through the rest of our living days on earth.

every minute of every hour of every day, week, month, year and all through the rest of our living days on earth.

Our Franciscan *"way of life"* is as much a part of ourselves as our skin. We don't zipper it on once a month for our regular meeting. It goes with us wherever we go.

It is exactly what we study in our Rule. Our Rule points the way very clearly and in full detail. We can't say too often that "our way" is the way of the Gospels.

Gospel reading is a MUST for Secular Franciscans. As we have said before we must read, read, read and ponder deeply what is read. Put it into action in the center of your life. Eat with it, sleep with it and walk with it. If you engross yourselves in this Gospel way it will be so much a part of you that you will react automatically when you are with others.

In particular, our brothers and sisters of the Catholic faith who have, as we have, received the sacred Body and Blood of Jesus Christ, must see in themselves the holy tabernacle in whom Christ dwells. In difficult situations we need to call this to mind and again and again ask ourselves, "How would Christ react to the Christ in this person? This question should be with us, too, in our encounters, pleasant or otherwise, with everyone.

This briefly, is what is meant by "going from Gospel to life, and from life to the Gospel."

Our Rule is to be a Gospel People

As we delve into the rich storehouse of the Scriptures, we become aware of the vastness of the Gospel message. Why? Because, it is the way of Jesus. As we progress in the understanding of the Gospels, we find we have an ever growing knowledge of Jesus.

Knowledge leads to intimacy, and intimacy brings an awareness of His LIVING PRESENCE. Filled with His living presence, we go back to the Gospels and read them more intelligently; because, now we know this Man, Jesus, and by knowing Him, we are coming to love Him more all the time.

Full of this growing love for Jesus we should now be ready to move away from our inner selves to share Him and His mission through our life in the Church.

We must never forget that first and foremost we are Catholics. Look at it this way; having fallen head over heels in love with Jesus, we SEEK His presence — we long to keep Him near us — we want to know His likes and dislikes, and we want to imitate Him. This feeling begins to show, or should show, in our actions when we come in contact with our brothers and sisters, because now we are acting for Him, in carrying out His mission in the world. We now should bring Christ of the Gospels to life so much so that He can be seen in us by all those we meet.

There is a parallel between our baptism through which we died to original sin, and were reborn in the grace of God and our profession as lay Franciscans. We die to the world and our own egos and are reborn in the humble, loving Christ; in His way, His truth and His life.

As Secular Franciscans we are committed to be Christ's hands, mouth, feet, HIMSELF, in the world. We are to be His heralds and workers, using our talents, opportunities, words, and actions to communicate His message, so that He walks and talks and comes to life through us, for all people.

This we do as members of our parish communities; thus, in a sense, we are rebuilding the Church as Francis was instructed to do by the Christ of San Damiano (see page 89).

As members of the Church (we are the body and life of the Church) we must be loyal and obedient to her proclamations, directives, teachings, doctrines and to our Holy Father, the Pope, our bishops, and our pastors.

We Secular Franciscans are Gospel people not for ourselves alone but for drawing others to our Gospel way, which is a closer union with Christ.

Our Rule is to strive for an Inner Conversion (Metanoia)

The basic thing to acknowledge in *metanoia* is that it is a sincere, dedicated and an ongoing attempt on the part of each of us individually to face up honestly to our own human weaknesses. Humility is all important. We all have our own opinions and we air them freely, but unfortunately we are loath to have them subjected to contradiction.

Some of our opinions are right, we know that, but some are not, and we are not always aware of that. And so, when someone is in disagreement with our opinion, we should courteously and respectfully listen to the ideas or way of the other person, though contrary to ours, and give it a fair-minded consideration. Never should we brush it aside as stupid.

Two of the most important aspects of *metanoia* are to be HUMBLE, and LISTEN.

"He who has ears let him hear," Jesus said.

Hear what?

Hear what the Gospel says about our relationship with people in the world. In the *First Book of Kings* we have this beautiful passage:

"Then the Lord said to Elijah 'Go outside and stand on the mountain before the Lord; the Lord will be passing by.' A strong and heavy wind was rending the mountains and crushing rocks before the Lord, but the Lord was not in the wind. After the wind there was an earthquake, but the Lord was not in the earthquake. After the earthquake there was fire, but the Lord was not in the fire. After the fire there was a tiny whispering sound. When he heard this Elijah hid his face in his cloak."

And of course the reason Elijah hid his face was that the whispering sound was God communicating with him.

Unless we are willing to listen we cannot possibly strive for the radical inner conversion, *metanoia*, that is an indispensable part of Franciscan formation.

Sometimes we need to be silent and listen to the other person's point of view — people have been known to learn something when they do. When we listen with our heart we find ourselves, and when we find ourselves we find Christ, and through Christ we find our brothers and sisters. By listening to our brothers and sisters we may just come full circle to where Christ is in everlasting life.

Our Rule is to have a Prayerful Life

Prayer is the motivating force, the electric current that turns on the light of Christ and starts our Grace-motors humming. The Grace is already there, but we need prayer to start its wheels turning.

This can begin, first thing in the morning, with a morning offering. By starting with this we will be taking God right into our day. St. Francis got to the point where he saw God in everything — a pebble, a worm, an animal, a tree, a flower, the sky, stars, sun, moon, clouds, a beggar, a king — you name it. Read his Canticle to Brother Sun, there's not much that he misses in that. Because of his association with all things that God created, everything became a prayer in his life.

Being in the Gospel way, we pluck a thought from St. Paul's letter to the Colossians *"Whether you eat or drink, or do anything else, do everything for God's glory."* Putting this into practice makes all of our ACTIONS prayers. Many beautiful words to God are great, but they are as hollow and evanescent as soap bubbles blown by a child if God is not in our actions. We have Jesus' own words to bear this out. *"Not everyone who says 'Lord, Lord' will enter the Kingdom of Heaven, but he who does the will of my Father."*

Most importantly, we have the Mass, the supreme prayer; then we have our daily Office — the Liturgy of the Hours is preferable or the 12 Our Fathers, 12 Hail Mary's, and 12 Glorias. Then you should have in your daily pattern, a period of meditation — a meeting of your mind, will and heart with your God — alone with Him. He is that kind of God. You can do this with Him confidently. He wants it! He wants each one of us to talk to Him. Oh, how blessedly lucky can we get?

Prayer is a MUST, without it in depth in our lives we are not only not forming ourselves as Franciscans, we are spiritually moribund.

With a prayer on his lips a derelict on skid row is greater in the eyes of God than a king on his throne without prayer. A king without prayer is like a soap bubble — resplendent outside, but hollow within.

Enough said! You take it from there. Work out your own prayer pattern or schedule for each day — you are adults. Do it the way that suits you best. This is what Article VIII is all about.

Our Rule says Follow the Way of Mary

Mary is the model of all the virtues, Faith, Hope, Love, Humility, Poverty, Chastity, Obedience, Gentleness, Kindness, Patience — you name them. Is there any virtue Mary did not radiate?

Is it any wonder St. Francis was her devoted son; that he put his "family" under her care.

Mary was a perfect example of Faith-In-Action in the unenlightened world were she lived. She had to grope her way through countless mysteries that were a part of her life.

1.   After her first gasp of fear and astonishment at the appearance of the Angel Gabriel, she uttered her sublime "Fiat."

2.   In trust and love she accepted Gabriel's words that her cousin Elizabeth, although of great age, was pregnant with John, and without questioning it she hastened to Elizabeth's house to help her in her time of need.

3.   Although her time of delivery was imminent, Mary went with Joseph to Bethlehem for the census, trusting in her heavenly Father to take care of the Virgin birth of His Son.

4.   Always ready to comply with the law and custom, she took the infant Jesus to the Temple for presentation to the Lord; and herself for purification — she, who was so pure.

5.   Without flinching she received the prophecy of Simeon that a sword would pierce her heart.

6.   In sorrow and joy, she sought and found her missing twelve-year-old Son in the Temple.

Our Rule is Simple Living

Again we touch on simple living, this time under the virtue of poverty.

Franciscan poverty alarms some people, but it needn't. What we're talking about is frugality and moderation, and reduced buying beyond our needs and increased sharing with others. It means a recognition of the fact that everything we have is not our own but on loan to us by God, for our use and to share with others. These gifts must be used for a GOOD purpose, in balance with all creation. When we find ourselves overstepping this balance, it is our responsibility to extricate ourselves in order to reach our poverty goal.

Possessions are not just material things but include our talents, our mind, affections, emotions and free will.

Freed from too much of anything, we are wide open to God, and to the needs of our disadvantaged brothers and sisters. It helps us to follow the advice of St. Elizabeth Ann Seton, "Live simply that others might simply live."

Certainly, living in the spirit of poverty, we will shun inordinate pride and greed. We are stewards, not owners. God forbid that He should have to tell us, because of our misuse of His gifts, "give an account of your stewardship for you can be stewards no longer."

Poverty is accepting what we have when we are unable to have more, and being thankful for what we have. It also means being glad when we are able to serve rather than be served.

It means we do not seek position, certainly not for self-interest; but when asked to fill a position we should accept it if we feel we are capable and have the necessary time to handle it. We then should apply ourselves to the very best of our ability, for the good of those we serve.

The more we give of ourselves to the acquisition of and preservation of property, the less there is to give to God and people, and the more we are possessed by things.

Gospel poverty is a detachment from material goods — a "we can take them or leave them" attitude.

Poverty of spirit makes us face up squarely to our *metanoia* — our stripping ourselves of worldliness, leaving us free to choose, in our

"Franciscan way of life," a COMMON SENSE attitude of simple living.

Our Rule is Chastity and Purity of Heart

Chastity is purity of heart and holiness as Jesus is holy.

Jesus said: Blessed are the clean of heart. Blessed are those whose actions attest to purity of heart in whatever field of endeavor, or whatever company. Blessed are the clean of mind.

Chastity is present where there is poverty of spirit and obedience to the Gospel way of Jesus.

Out of purity of heart comes not only chastity in physical living, but Christ-centered love, which in its cleanness does not admit carelessness or neglect of the dignity of the human person.

The purity of Christ in our hearts, if it is true and deep-seated, does not allow us to view with complacency poverty in the world, nor disobedience. These virtues are inseparable in a Franciscan's simple way of life. The point of simple living is to put aside everything that can come between us and God.

Chastity is the purity of love that comes from the heart of Jesus. It reflects the two great Commandments: "You shall love your God with all your heart, and your neighbor as yourself ..." It is not concerned alone with the sixth and ninth Commandments, but embraces all the Commandments. It is a purity that has no flaw, as the Blessed Virgin Mary is flawless.

Here are a few examples on what we should reflect on:

How do we feel about indecent jokes, TV programs, books and movies?

How do I express myself through the way I dress and what I eat and drink?

What does my house and the way I keep my room say about me?

How do I spend my money?

We have to confront ourselves by asking questions like these and give ourselves serious answers. If we do not like our answers we have an indication that change may be needed.

Our Rule is to live in Community

In this Gospel way there are responsibilities. Our first is to people — the responsibility to be friendly, to serve, to lead others towards Christ. Then we must be fair, unbiased and unprejudiced and accept humbly what we have.

Franciscan community living is not just mingling at the meetings. It involves much give and take.

All people are our brothers and sisters, each is a unique child of our heavenly Father. With all people, a Franciscan should be gentle, peaceful, unassuming, courteous, basically humble and respectful to all.

Each person is equal in this sense. For example, one of low intellect who uses this intellect the best he can in order to bring it to its highest potential, will probably never achieve great things; nevertheless, in attaining one hundred percent of his potential, he is on a level of achievement with the genius who likewise develops his capabilities to one hundred percent.

It is important, where we can, to help less advantaged persons learn to stand on their own feet. This gives them a sense of their own dignity and self-worth. A sense of dignity is everyone's God-given right.

All this is a part of a Franciscan's responsibility, to be heralds of the great King, and take a hand in making God's Kingdom come on earth.

The opportunities to serve are right where we live. At all times we should be alert and ready to serve in the arena of our own individual capabilities and talents.

We must not envy what someone else is able to do. It takes many different talents, small, mediocre and great to build up the body of Christ. A fingernail is not nearly as big or noticeable as a strong arm, but it is just as necessary a part of the whole body.

Anyone who follows Christ, the perfect man, is bound to become a more perfect man or woman.

Our Rule is to be a People of Justice

Are our judgments just? Do we often jump to conclusions? Do we misjudge something said or done? Do we resent something that does not agree with what we think? Is that just?

Do we listen with respect to other people's opinions; weigh them pro and con; accept or reject courteously?

Are we just in our attitude towards priests. Do we show marked favoritism or only see faults in one we don't particularly like? Do we ever look for the good in him?

Does the testimony of our lives indicate we are in the forefront in promoting justice as this Article advocates? Do we look down on some people? Do we refuse to forgive?

Do we participate in elections? How? Do we study the candidates from all angles? Or do we latch onto one single thing we like, or don't like? Do we always vote for one party because that is what we have always done? Do we vote as we think God would want us to vote on certain issues? Do we try to decide honestly from all angles which candidate, in God's eyes, would be best for all the people and for the country?

Perhaps in our examination of conscience we could look back over the events of the day, especially the difficult ones and ask ourselves, how did I react in that situation? Did I react with justice? Did I think of my own desires only, or did I think of the other person's needs?

There is a marvelous illustration of justice and how it works in the story of the "wolf of Gubbio."

The wolf was hungry. He had a God-given right to food. Since no one gave it to him, he went after it wherever he could find it, even when he violated others rights. He was feared and hated. St. Francis, ever the peacemaker, took a hand in the situation and approached the wolf with courtesy, respect and compassion, and won from him the promise of a surcease of his predatory ways if the townsfolk would supply him with the food he needed. They agreed. Thereafter he roamed from door to door with wagging tail instead of snarling fangs and accepted happily and peacefully the food given to him. When he died the townsfolk felt they had lost a friend. They mourned him. Thus was justice and brotherly love served between the townsfolk and brother wolf.

May we implore God, the Just Judge, to impart to us the wisdom to be Christ-like in our judgments, actions, and speech.

Our Rule is to Foster Dignity in all People

"Let them esteem work both as a gift and as a sharing in the creation, redemption, and service of the human community."

Psalm 128 says, in part, *"O blessed are those who fear the Lord and walk in his ways. By the labor of your hands you shall eat. You will be happy and prosper."* Thus, people from ancient times have regarded the putting of bread on their own tables by their own hands as highly desirable and praiseworthy; giving them a sense of dignity and worth. The work of one person can be of tremendous good to many people.

Here is one example: an employee doing his job on a trash collection truck is certainly doing God's work, because he is doing an important job of renewing the face of the earth. His work, as all good work, is a sharing in the creation of the Father, a sharing in the ongoing apostolate of the Son who left it to us to carry on after He ascended into Heaven. It is not just for our own welfare, but, because the end result helps many other people in so many ways.

A cheerful, conscientious worker has the love of the Holy Spirit in what he is doing.

To use one's talents and develop them for our own good and the good of our neighbor is to bring glory to God.

In anything right we undertake to do, we should do to the very best of our ability. We should take pride in a job well done and be grateful to God for it, because it is doing His work.

A Franciscan should always be aiming at perfection, always ready to go the extra mile — that's the Gospel way.

It is in our environment, whether we are working or retired; in the home, neighborhood, parish or wherever, that we move on our way towards salvation. This is our world where we live; how well we perform in this world will determine the progress we are making towards salvation.

We should ask ourselves and meditate on how did the life of Jesus, Mary, and Joseph, the Apostles and St. Francis show us the way to Live?

Now, I will conclued with these little anecdotes: Which is more important: sweeping a floor, or singing a hymn; a priest preparing his homily, or a little boy studying his homework; a senator working on the laws of the land, or a mother baking bread?

We have reached the end of my dissertation on the Rule for now. I hope you have gained some insight of our Rule.

Notes

Notes

*"Your Franciscan way of life begins in,
is nurtured on, and blossoms out
of your Franciscan meeting.
This is your community life."*

Monthly Meetings

One of the most frustrating things I have encountered is the importance of the monthly meetings in dedicating yourself to the "Franciscan Way of Life."

The Secular Franciscan Order is not just another spiritual organization, club or society; not just another undertaking to tack on to other spiritual things a person is already involved in. Problems arise when you are involved in, for example, the Charismatic movement. Good! You have good reasons and you tell us what those reasons are; they all seem good. Then you reach a point in your profession and find a conflict. Now, what is happening? Are you satisfied now to be a Franciscan? Yes, but ... You become restless and hear members talking about committing yourself to the Franciscan way of life — to its obligations.

Where is your loyalty, your dedication to this Franciscan way you were so excited about before. Now you are allowing another spirituality, good though it my be, to push it aside.

The Franciscan way of life cannot be pushed aside. Once you go through the ceremony of profession, where you stand up there in that deeply religious ceremony during Mass and solemnly pledge before God to live under the Rule and Constitutions of the Secular Franciscan Order, you assume for life this obligation. You cannot take it off like a removable garment so that you can put on another garment you prefer for the moment. You cannot because it is not a removable garment. It is a part of you just as surely as your skin. You cannot zipper into and out of your skin or the Franciscan Order. It goes right along with you wherever you go. True Franciscanism requires sacrifices, at times, for the good of your fraternity and of the Franciscan Order.

The Eucharistic ministry is an edifying and necessary work in our parishes, but if you are a Secular Franciscan and want to become a Eucharistic minister, in my opinion, you have an obligation to schedule your times of serving *around* the day of your regular Franciscan meeting. Make it known to the person in charge of your schedule that such-and-such day is the day of your Franciscan meeting and you cannot serve that day — any other day, yes, happily and gladly; but, not your Franciscan meeting day.

Your Franciscan way of life begins in, is nurtured on, and blossoms out of your Franciscan meeting. This is your community life. Only for a good and acceptable reason should you skip a regular meeting. There are times, such as health problems and family matters, that you skip a regular meeting, but to do it month after month because you prefer something else is a violation of your solemn profession promise. A sincere, dedicated, loyal Secular Franciscan will not tolerate in him or herself such a violation.

Without our regular monthly meetings, our Franciscan Order will come to a dead end and cease to exist. We all owe it to God, St. Francis, and our brothers and sisters of our fraternity, who NEED our presence at the meetings, not to let that happen.

"Franciscans cannot stop at the bottom of the hill of Calvary."

Franciscan Commitment

On a beautiful, sunny day along the countryside around Assisi, a young man astride his horse was cantering along the dirt road. He was singing lustily and joyfully as the road wound in beautiful fashion between tall, stately trees. He came into a clearing and was brought up short. There, just off the road in plain sight, stood a pitiable figure of a man. He was bent, dressed in ragged garments, his body emaciated and covered with sores, his eyes were deep set with a mysterious, burning light in them. The man was a leper.

The young rider stared at him in horror and started to edge his horse around him on the extreme outer edge of the road, but the horse stood still and refused to budge. The young man was troubled. A force within him, against his will, urged him to get down from his horse and approach the leper. The impulse was so strong he found himself reluctantly dismounting, and literally, dragging his feet, he walked over to the leper. Then he, through some power outside him, threw his arms about the loathsome figure and embraced him. The embrace was weak at first, then with warmth and strength, and to his amazement he found his loathing give way to a peace beyond anything he had ever experienced. A fullness of the joy of living suffused him as he mounted his horse and started off down the road. He looked back and uttered a cry of astonishment, there was no one in sight, and where the leprous figure had stood there was no one.

This was Francis of Assisi, a man who would become one of the greatest saints of the Church.

Francis closed his eyes. He recalled the burning, mysterious light in the man's deep-set eyes. Awed and humbled he bowed his head over his horse's mane. He rode away then, his lips moving in prayer. "Lord," he said over and over, "O Lord, my God and my all."

We, like Francis, in our Franciscan commitment should recognize that we have been called by God to this way of life. Though we are not confronted with the same dramatic confrontation that Francis had we are living in a similar situation in the world, with its uncertainty and critical challenges. We are members of his fraternity and our goal is exactly the same as his was, namely, union with Christ. We know that Francis, so wholly committed, asked Jesus to grant him the extraordinary gift that while he was still alive on earth he might feel in his body the pain Jesus felt during His Passion, and that he might experience in his heart the overwhelming, burning love Jesus had for all of mankind.

After he had embraced the leper, Francis remarked, "When I came away from the leper, what seemed bitter to me was changed to a sweetness of spirit and body."

When we became his followers we also set our feet on the way which leads to forgetfulness of self. It brings about a steady, progressive embracing of the selfless love of Jesus Christ. In order to achieve this we will have,so to speak, the opportunity many times, to embrace a "leper," from whom we will have the tendency to shrink from; but, after we have accomplished the embrace, we will be left with a feeling of joy that can only be known for what it is — a personal encounter with Christ.

This way we have chosen is not a way where we unlock a door, open it, step through, and there we are. Oh no! At times we wonder what we have gotten ourselves into. We may wonder how we can follow the way of Francis? He was a great saint, but Francis was Francis, and I am me, and you are you. Each one of us is a special individual chosen by God.

We cannot wait until everything is all together before we believe in Jesus. We accept Jesus and move along His way as He reveals Himself to us. We reach out to the possibilities of life and see where they lead. There is no other way for the Franciscan to go; no other truth to seek; no other life to live than in Jesus.

The way to Jesus requires discipline. When we choose to follow Francis we did not accept the fly-by-night people who would give us "instant" religion and quick conversion. This is not for the followers of Francis or for that matter any Catholic — the comfort of painless growth without the cross. The contentment of being "saved" and having to do nothing more is not for us. It is not for us to have mere human sensitivity that can be a mask for self-centeredness. Franciscans cannot stop at the bottom of the hill of Calvary.

There will be times when we will be weary and feel like we are walking through a dark forest, but we will go on and pass a rise and come into a clearing. We will sit down on green grass to rest and see stars shining overhead and we will feel a sense of peace and exhilaration. We will laugh as we look back over the way we have come. As we sit there on the cool green grass, there will come over us a sixth sense of His presence near us — and we will bow our heads in reverence as did Francis over his horse's mane and know that this, indeed, is it! This is our way and we are not alone — never alone. We know that time after time we may feel lost and uncertain of what is ahead, but we will know that we are not alone. We will not turn back, because we have Christ at our side. And, we have each other — brothers and sisters who walk forward together in the way of St. Francis of Assisi.

From now on we are not satisfied with anything less. We have an urge to become more knowledgeable about Jesus. We have an urge to make friends with Him and become intimate with Him. We have an urge to aspire, weak as it may be for us insignificant people, to the heroic spirituality of Francis. The same spirituality that led him to the mountain of La Verna where he met Christ, as it were, on the hill of Calvary.

Speaking of La Verna, let us dwell on that episode in Francis' life when Francis on the day, two years before his death, in the hushed, cathedral-like setting of Mount La Verna, he was kneeling absorbed in prayer. Francis came out of his meditative absorption to become suddenly aware of a shining seraph, an angel of God, looking at him. The seraph was in the form of a man fixed in terrible pain to a cross. Wordlessly they stared at each other, the seraph and the living being. Then the vision disappeared.

As Francis stood rooted to the spot trying to understand the meaning of the suffering apparition, he felt a sharp tingling in both hands and feet and in his side, then excruciating stabs of pain from those regions of his body. In wonderment he stared at his hands and saw forming there prints as of nails. They were so realistic that they looked as though there were indeed iron nails in his hands, and this was true also in his feet.

Actually these were his own flesh which had taken on the shape and color of iron nails. He felt a warm moisture at his side and touched it and his hand came away bloody.

Francis was at great pains during the remaining two years of his life to conceal this gift of God from other people lest he become vain, but he was not altogether able to do this. At his death those present could clearly see and touch his wounds.

His prayers were answered. He felt in his body the pain Jesus endured in His Passion, and he experienced in his heart the enormous, burning love Jesus has for all mankind.

Let us now lift our minds in prayer.

O Jesus

Shake me O Jesus, loose my rigidity;
Warm me, O Jesus, inflame my frigidity.

Humble me, Lord, and subdue my conceit;
Repentant and poor, let me kneel at your feet.

From the lure of the world, please give me a shove;
Let my heart burn with the fire of your love.

Let me follow your way and not crave any other;
Let me never forget every man is my brother.

Protect me, I pray you, from earth's wiles and charms;
Let me die, O my Jesus, safe in your arms.

*"... it is a Church prayer,
a liturgical prayer."*

The Secular Franciscan's
Daily Office

The Franciscan daily office or any Office, priestly, religious, etc. should be said for the intention of the Church (Keep in mind that we are the Church as well as those in the Vatican and all the hierarchy). While you actually say your Office which is most of the time alone, you are never really saying it alone. There is no time when somewhere someone in the world is not also saying an Office for the Church, thus, it is a Church prayer, a liturgical prayer.

According to the SFO Rule, the members of the Secular Franciscan Order are to join in liturgical prayer in one of the forms proposed by the Church, reliving the mysteries of Christ.

Here are some suggestions regarding how the Secular Franciscans may fulfill this responsibility:

1. Morning and evening prayer from the Liturgy of the Hours, either in common or in private. This celebration is preferred at the fraternity meeting.

2. A shortened form of the Liturgy of the Hours

3. The Little Office of the Blessed Virgin Mary, which is compatible with the structure of the Liturgy of the Hours.

4. The Office of the Passion written by St. Francis of Assisi.

5. The Office of the Twelve Our Fathers in one of its many versions that have been enriched with short biblical readings. This form of prayer still thrives in many parts of the world, and has become a traditional expression of Secular Franciscan prayer. It is a useful way of praying in everyday circumstances.

6. Other forms of liturgical prayer, approved by the spiritual assistant or by one's spiritual director, as long as they contain psalms, or their equivalent with Scripture readings and prayers.

7. Special Prayer forms for the liturgical seasons, for example:

    a) The Way of the Cross during Lent (with Scripture readings).

    b) The Rosary or Franciscan Crown during May and October with Scripture readings.

There are books like the "Secular Franciscan Companion" to help you with the meditation of the Office.

But you should keep in mind each day the intentions of the Church, which are the intentions of Christ. This brings us still closer to Him because we are praying for what He wants. You should be very faithful to this devotion of praying the daily Office.

No, they do not have to be prayed at those specified times. You can arrange them to suit your own convenience.

A Secular Franciscan's Life of Prayer

The Secular Franciscans aim should be, at all times, a closer and closer union with Christ. This can be done in many ways, but there is no way better than by talking directly to Christ. We have considered some of these ways: daily Mass and Holy Communion when possible; a Spiritual Communion when you can't make Mass; the Franciscan Crown (rosary); There are many ways that are personal to each one of us — morning and evening, before meals and after and walking the "Way of the Cross" with Jesus down the aisles of a church. There are mental tête-à-têtes with God — Sacred readings inspired by the sight of a flower, a leaf, a cloud, the sound of music, or a bird, of laughter, of weeping, of any beauty, any kindness, any compassion, any reaching out; in the blossoming of any such buds anywhere in God's creation, from our heart to the heart of God.

"Come," we say to Jesus — at any time, day or night. "Come into my heart, my soul and my thoughts. Jesus, if you are in my thoughts, you are in my heart, and in my soul, and in my life. If you are in my life, then I am truly united with you, and that is what I want, my life united with the real presence of my Jesus."

Now, none of these is obligatory. You and I choose what best suits each one of us in our endeavor to bring Christ into the very inmost center of our life, and, no prayer, and no attendance at a spiritual service, or gathering must ever interfere with one's obligations to those in our care, or those in need around us. If it is a question of should I say my prayers right now, or should I take care of household task that needs to be done for the care of someone, the latter takes precedence always. The household task is your prayer. If it is a question of, should I attend this religious service, or should I take care of this sick person who has no one else to care for him or her, then the answer, of course, is self-evident. Remember what Jesus said, *"As long as you do it to one of these, the least of my brethren ..."* These actions are prayers. This is union with Christ, to the Christ who is in this person I am helping — from the Christ who is in me.

Notes

*"Let us begin, for we have
done nothing up till now."*

The Franciscan Life Style is the Gospel way

What should be the life style of a Secular Franciscan?

The answer is simple; simple for each person in accordance with his particular circumstance in life. But, regardless of the circumstances, we are "little" people, who should wish for nothing better than to be childlike imitators of Christ's humility, meekness, gentleness, kindness, and tolerance. Each one of us should be determined to serve rather than be served. We should slip quietly into the least desirable place, leaving the best for someone else.

Childlike and humble, a Secular Franciscan should be open to God's word. He should be obedient to His commands; all of them without exception; receptive to His Sacraments; loyal to His Church, holding in respect all forms of life and all created things.

In a spirit of penance, a Secular Franciscan, who is a member of the order of penitents, should be willingly cheerful to adapt to any and all kinds of circumstances. For Example: to our living quarters, the weather, and to temperature conditions beyond our control. We can accomplish it in a spirit like that of our Seraphic Father Francis who sweated and shivered with a song of joy on his lips.

In a spirit of penance there can be joy and a freedom that allows us to relate ourselves closely to our Suffering Servant, Jesus. The cornerstone on which we build our simple life style "is Jesus." His sense of values should be ours.

Our life style embraces obedience; our wills united to His will; an optimistic outlook; patience in sufferings, hurts, trials, frustrations that cannot be avoided and which can be redemptively united to His sufferings. It is a great way to draw closer to Him and this should be our chief purpose in life. Are not our crosses feather-light compared to His? Touching our hand to His could stab one's heart with a thrill of joy that could desensitize pain better than any man-made painkiller.

These are some thoughts on which a Secular Franciscan can build his life style. There can be much more to it depending on each individual's outlook and dedication. And, it can be so deep down satisfyingly and worthwhile!

Our way is the "Gospel Way"

We Franciscans are engaged in a life style that seeks a goal of perfection through the "Gospel Way" — "The Franciscan Way of Life." In essence, as Francis said, "Let us begin for we have done nothing up to now." This is rather earthshaking! We should listen to that message. It doesn't mean we've done nothing in the past, it means we must strive to do even better in all things to get to that goal of perfection.

Look at man's struggles with earthly things; by the grace of God, after having struggled for some time, he was able to invent a square wheel, which bumped along on every turn; then, as time went on, he came up with a round wheel, and later on he put rubber on the wheel which helped it to be quiet and roll smoothly.

We can look back on our spiritual climb, make a chart to see how we have bumped along over the years. Have we gotten there yet — perfection? Well, keep on trying, you won't miss if you follow the "Gospel Way."

There is no better Gospel passage to follow than the one from St. Paul: *"I do not claim that I have already succeeded or have already become perfect. I keep going on to win the prize for which Christ Jesus has already won me to himself. Of course, my brothers, I really do not think that I have already won it; the one thing I do, however, is to forget what is behind me and do my best to reach for what is ahead. So I run straight toward the goal in order to win the prize which is God's call though Christ Jesus to the life above."* (Philippians 3: 12-14).

"St. Francis' way was to 'Go to the Gospel.'"

Franciscan Spirituality

The theme today is Franciscan Spirituality, based on St. Francis' deep conviction that God is our good Father. He is not a Father we obey because of fear of punishment. He is a generous and benign Father whom we want to obey because we know He loves us and we want Him to know that we love Him.

Franciscan spirituality is a particular way of striving for perfection. The goal of all spirituality's, be they Benedictine, Dominican, Franciscan, or whatever, are the same, but the means of reaching the goal are different. They are alike, as human beings are alike, but they are different, as each human being is different. The difference lies in the way of life established by their leaders. The Franciscan main emphasis is on the Gospels and God's love. It is the true and powerful message that St. Francis found. Members of the Secular Franciscan Order should aim, gradually, but persistently and sincerely to develop this spirit of God's great love in themselves.

The Franciscan way is a lofty way. Is it then, superior to other ways? The answer is no. Benedictine, Dominican and all spirituality is lofty. Each person, then, is free to choose and follow the spirituality he prefers. All are equally good and Christ is the focal point of all of them.

St. Francis' way was to, "Go to the Gospel." This is the way Christ taught us. "In the Gospels we find our way, our truth and our life."

We have said that Francis thought of God, most of all, as our good Father. Christ in the Gospels, particularly that of St. John, was continually calling upon His Father. Everything He did was for His Father and with the aid of his Father. We have this happy truth to cherish — God is Christ's Father — God is our Father — so, joyfully we can say, "Christ is our brother!"

The greatest thing God could give us is life — and through this human life we receive a sharing in His life. God became man so that man might share in His life, having His love — reborn in His love so that we are able to see His love in everything, in all of creation, in all creatures, and in particular, in all men.

Francis rediscovered the powerful truth in the Gospels that Christ is not only God, but also, He is man! He is a true man with a human body, emotions, feelings — "a man," the Gospels say, *"like us in everything but sin."*

God's love draws us to Himself, through Christ. As God the Father would lovingly enfold Christ, His Son, in His arms, so too, would He enfold us, His children. The truth of this thrilled Francis with an overpowering joy.

A sad note we see too often is that man, with his free will, can and does refuse this gift of God — this love and grace beyond our imagining. Man in his arrogant stupidity can revert to what he was to begin with — nothing — or worse than nothing. *"It were better for that man,"* Jesus said at one point, *"if he had not been born."*

To reject God's love is the greatest of all the tragedies of life. But, it is a tragedy of choice.

The God-Man Jesus is our great hope. In God's eternal plan from the beginning, there was a human nature that would embody the fullness and perfection of God's own goodness and love. This human nature was Christ. In Christ we have a meeting place of uncreative love with created love. As God, Christ is uncreative Love. As man He offers to His Father a perfect created love. As God He brings the infinite love of His Father down to us, and as man He gives back to the Father a perfect human love.

God, from the beginning, had billions of images of Christ in His eternal plan. At the top of the list is Mary, to whom Francis had a very deep devotion. And, below her on the list are the billions of images of Christ. Who are they? It is you and I — children of God by His gift, living a life that shares the life of God.

God, as the all-seeing God, has deep compassion towards mankind, but when He Himself became man, He backed up this compassion with His own self-experienced day-by-day living. He felt and shared our human existence. He understands our human problems because He is a human Himself. He ate and drank with his friends and felt cold, heat, pain, joy and sorrow. His humanity rubbed elbows with our humanity — our problems, He knows from a first-hand experience.

God then, having united us human beings with Christ in our shared human nature, also unites us by giving us a share in His own divine nature. How wonderful this is, our unity with Christ and God our Father; His own kind of life, to our human nature, making us supernatural. This also lifts our Love for God far above any human love. Our love for Him becomes supernatural love. This is a pure gift. God does not love us, because we are good and holy. We become good and holy because God loves us.

By the sin of Adam and Eve we are born dead to the eternal love of God, but as St. Paul says, *"God's plan was to restore all things in Christ."* Christ willingly became a member of the human race, and in that capacity, glorified beyond measure, the fact that He also is the Son of God. He performed the supreme sacrifice and thereby lifted us body and soul, right up to God.

To be a Franciscan is to strive unceasingly to absorb into our day-by-day living these joyful truths.

"The Christian calling is a calling to evangelize."

Evangelizing is the Apostolate of the Laity

Our role as evangelizers has been emphasized all along for us by what, we as Franciscans, have been studying over the years. It is the substance of the section of Vatican II, "Apostolate of the Laity," which states, one of its goals is to intensify apostolic activity throughout the laity. "Where priests are few," it says, "the Church would barely exist without a functioning laity."

Participation of the laity carries into the Church's apostolic activities those aims of the Church to spread Christ's kingdom. This is always the starting point for spiritual activity. From there we go to involvement by us, the laity, in Christ's saving redemption, relating the whole world to Christ. This is evangelizing.

The Christian calling is a calling to evangelize. We of the laity have this right and duty. It is centered squarely on Christ and nourished by the Sacraments.

The Holy Spirit gives special gifts to each individual, who in turn, has the duty and freedom to exercise these gifts under the guidance of our pastor for the building up of the Church. You will find a very similar statement in our Rule.

Lay apostolic success must begin with union with Christ, aided by the liturgies of the Church.

Through faith, hope and love, lay people should permeate all their activities with the spirit of Christ.

Since we Franciscans follow the Gospel Way we have the freedom to exercise through faith the Word of God. We find God and are able to seek His will and see Christ in all men, and make sound judgments on the true meaning and value of temporal things. We are then freed from bondage of riches and are able to look for everlasting values. In life's trials, it gives us the hope and belief that the sufferings of the present cannot be compared to the glory to come.

Our purpose is to respect and promote the welfare of all people, putting aside what is vicious and deceitful and shun pretense, jealousies, and disparaging remarks. This is the way to attract people to Christ, and perhaps in our case, to our Franciscan way of life.

Following the poor Jesus, lay people should not be depressed in want or proud in plenty. They should seek to please God, not man. Their spirituality is centered on their particular circumstance in life, health and abilities. They work out of that center.

Each person's talents and gifts have been given to him by God; specifically, because God thought them suitable to that person. These gifts and talents should be cultivated diligently, along with social virtues such as justice, courtesy, etc.

The perfect model of these virtues is the Blessed Mother. As Vatican II says, everyone should have an authentic devotion to the Blessed Mother.

"We have been endowed with a body to enable us to work;
an intellect to enable us to know what it is we need to do;
a free will to spur us on and an immortal soul to lift us
up higher than ourselves."

Secular Franciscans and the Holy Spirit

Why is Pentecost the birthday of the Church of Jesus Christ? Why not December 25, the day Christ was born?

Because, until Pentecost there was no "Good News" to proclaim — only the distressing tale of a man who had preached, died in ignominy, and was buried. It was the end, or so it seemed, at that moment.

But suddenly things began to happen. He burst forth from the tomb, ALIVE and forty days later He ascended into heaven in His glorified body. After His Ascension came the electrifying fulfillment of His promise, when on Pentecost Sunday the Holy Spirit came down with a roar of wind and a flash of flames and the "Good News" became a living reality; a message of faith and hope and love to be proclaimed to all the world. This is exactly what the apostles and disciples did with zest and zeal that first Pentecost day, when 3,000 people believed. That was the birth of the Church — those 3,000 people, the people of God, the Church. They were then, as we are now, the Church.

What has this to do with our Secular Franciscan Order?

The Holy Spirit floods us with grace — a pure gift. We can't buy it. We can't earn it. We receive it gratis. And that is where the parable begins to have meaning for us, because, through the grace of God, we can begin to develop our God-given talents.

Every living person is blessed with a talent or talents. To strive to develop these to the best of our ability brings a smile and a joyful "Well done" from God.

Let no person say he or she has no talent. God has gifted each one of us with something special.

For most of us, our abilities are not all that great. But, ability we have, because as human beings, created by God, we have been endowed with a body to enable us to work, an intellect to enable us to know what it is we need to do and a free will to spur us on and an immortal soul to lift us up higher than ourselves.

Irradiated by the grace of the Holy Spirit, we accept from the Holy Spirit the gift of Faith. We believe in God and receive the gift of Hope — we can reach beyond our human capacity to a share in that which is Divine. And, we receive the gift of Love which is the Holy Spirit within us.

As Franciscans we accept the gifts the Spirit gives us with gratitude. Most of us do not ask for greater gifts. The more spectacular ones of the Holy Spirit, which are His alone to give are the gift of tongues, discernment, prophecy and the supernatural. Most of us, humbly and obediently, are satisfied to receive the "Seven Gifts of the Holy Spirit" which are ours for the asking — and ask we should. These are ordinary gifts, if any gift from the Holy Spirit can be called ordinary. I'm not talking about phenomenal gifts, I'm talking about the basic gifts of Wisdom, Understanding, Knowledge, Fortitude, Counsel, Piety, and Fear of the Lord.

First of all let us ask for the gift of "Wisdom," which is a beginning. Let us pray intensely for this one, which, when God told King Solomon he could ask for whatever he desired, Solomon replied that he would like Wisdom so that he could rule his people wisely and justly. God was enormously pleased with his reply. Wisdom is to know the way, the truth and the life of Jesus that He gave to us when He walked the earth.

From the gift of "Wisdom," we can move on to the gift of "Understanding." With this gift we receive a greater understanding of our relationship, as humans, to a God who is our Loving Father, our Savior and our Love and Consolation.

With the gift of "Understanding" we move on to the gift of "Knowledge" where we have a greater knowledge of Jesus in our lives. We are bringing Him alive out of the pages of the Gospels into our daily living. We are now in the position of what St. Paul was talking about when he said, ... *"we have complete victory through Him who loves us! For I am certain that nothing can separate us from His love: neither death nor life, neither angels nor other heavenly rulers or powers; neither the present nor the future; neither the world above nor the world below — there is nothing in all creation that will ever be able to separate us from the love of God which is ours through Christ Jesus our Lord." (Rom. 8: 37-39)*

The gift of "Knowledge" is given to us so that we understand what his message is for each one of us individually, so we may grasp the how, the when and the wherefore of His message as we live day by day in this our secular world of existence.

Next is the gift of "Fortitude" which gives us the courage, and stamina to stick to our convictions, not only through good times; but in particular, through bad times — times of heartbreak, trials, frustrations, sufferings, disappointments, and depression of the spirit. We are fixed, firm and immovable, set in concrete in His love. No pain, no sickness, no heartache, no frustration, no ridicule or put-down; nothing can take it from us. It is ours to have and to hold, and this powerful fact is implemented in us by our gift of "Fortitude."

With the gift of "Counsel" we are now able to transmit this "Good News," we have come to understand. We can show other people how to evangelize, not necessarily by words or preaching, but simply by our example. Our light now is shining clearly before men so that we can, through wisdom, understanding and knowledge, have the necessary know-how to share Christ's way and truth. This is our gift of "Counsel."

The gift of "Counsel" is bolstered by the gift of "Piety" as we reach towards the level of St. Francis (at least we are striving towards it).

Thomas of Celano said of him: "He was a man so steeped in love for Jesus Christ that he had Jesus in his eyes, Jesus in his ears, Jesus in his mouth, Jesus in his hands, Jesus in every member of his body." This is what we strive for through the gift of "Piety."

And finally, the gift of "Fear of the Lord." This one may seem difficult. Fear of the Lord? I don't fear the Lord. What is it, to fear the Lord? To some it is one thing, to others it is something else. To my understanding, it is love, a deep-seated, pervasive love of God that makes us fear, above everything else, our own human weaknesses that could make us vulnerable to influences that could come between us and His love. It is the fear that unless we are constantly on our toes spiritually we may separate ourselves from Him, and the fear that something we might do or neglect to do, or say, will hurt Him who has already been so terribly hurt by all of us down through the centuries.

It is like that dear, lovable, rough fisherman, Peter, who hurt Him. Remember that day when the cock crowed and Jesus looked at him and that look stabbed deep down into Peter's heart and he stood there aghast at what he had done, his head dropped down to his chest and he remained there sobbing like a little boy who realizes he had done something awful that hurt his beloved father.

What Peter felt was not fear. It was contrition born of true love — deep, deep love. Fear of the Lord is such a love.

All this is ours because this is what it is to be a Franciscan and walk the Way of the Gospel. We are rising out of our mundane drabness and lifted high above our own poor abilities into the realm of the Divine.

It is thrilling and a real marvel that this should be ours; we who are just little ordinary people, the minor brothers and sisters, the poverelli. We do not aspire to perform center stage under a spotlight. We are content to use our little natural talents in a supernatural way. This is the tremendous message of St. Francis.

God grant that we use our minds and hearts and wills to bring the Fear of the Lord to a very pinnacle in our lives so that God can call out to us joyfully some day and say, *"Well done, good and faithful servant! Said his master. You have been faithful in managing small amounts, so I will put you in charge of large amounts. Come on in and share my happiness! (Matt. 25: 21).*

Prayer to the Holy Spirit

Holy Spirit, giver of life and light,
Help us who take part in any gathering
to serve you both in the Church
and in the world.
Grant that we may think honestly and
speak wisely, and make us ready
to listen to others.
Bestow on us and on all your people
your bond of unity and peace; that all may
know us as Jesus' followers,
because we have love for one another.
May we, with one heart and one voice,
glorify the eternal Trinity,
God blest forever more.

Amen.

REFLECTIONS OF A SECULAR FRANCISCAN

"... the Crown of Seven Joys of Mary"

What is Mary to us as Franciscans?

We know that Christ is the Head of the Mystical Body, the Church. We know that Mary is the mother of Christ. Therefore, Mary is the mother of the Mystical Body, which is all of us. Mary is our Mother.

A deep love for Mary is a characteristic mark of the entire Franciscan Order. St. Francis looked upon her as a special advocate and protectoress of his Order. He prayed to her before he said his breviary each hour. In countless instances during his life we find evidence of his devotion and respect for her, the mother of his idolized Lord and Savior, Jesus Christ.

St. Francis placed his three orders under her special patronage. The poor little church outside Assisi, which he helped to restore, the "Portiuncula," or "The Little Portion," he dedicated to her, naming it "Our Lady of the Angels." He made it the mother church of his entire Order and St. Clare took her vows as the head of his second order, the Poor Clares, within it's hallowed interior.

One of the followers of St. Francis, long ago, founded the devotion of the Franciscan Rosary which we know as the Franciscan Crown. This rosary is devoted to the Crown of Seven Joys of Mary. They are:

1. The Annunciation.
2. The Visitation.
3. The Birth of the Lord.
4. The Adoration of the Magi *and/or* The Presentation and Purification.
5. The Finding of the Child Jesus in the Temple.
6. The Resurrection of our Lord.
7. Her Assumption and Coronation into Heaven.

The method is: start the Crown with the first decade; recite the 7 decades and at the end say 2 hail Marys for the 72 years of Mary's life on earth. Finally say one Our Father, Hail Mary and Glory Be for the intentions of the Holy Father.

In this Crown we rejoice with Mary in her joys. But, we should not forget her Crown of Thorns — the sword that pierced her heart. With deep gratitude we should remember her agony as she followed her Son's journey to Calvary and remember how her heart broke when she saw His body slump in death on the cross.

"Oh Jesus ...
I offer you my prayers,
works, joys and sufferings"

Morning Offering

First of all let us get in the practice, each day if at all possible, of reading a little bit from the Gospels or other spiritual or Franciscan works. We can't emphasize too much that the Franciscan way is the Gospel way. Unless we believe this and act on it we will never really be Franciscans.

But, aside from that, let us try to cultivate a good habit — the habit of giving our pains, our heartaches, our annoyances, our rebuffs, etc., etc., etc., to Jesus, all day long.

I am writing here the Morning Offering — if any of you do not know it already:

Oh Jesus, through the Immaculate Heart of Mary, I offer you my prayers, works, joys and sufferings of this day, in union with the sacrifice of the Mass throughout the world, in reparation for my sins and the sins of all mankind, for the intentions of all our associates, and in particular for the general intention of the Holy Father for this month.

Now, every morning, as soon as you get out of bed, focus your mind on Jesus and say this little offering. There are other versions of this prayer that you can use.

Then, throughout the day, every single time something pops up to annoy you, or hurt you in any way, give it to Jesus. You could say, "Jesus, I offer this to you," or you could use your own words, but try to picture, or better still, sense the presence of Jesus in the room.

I am sure that at first you will forget it right and left; so, if you need a reminder, write it down on a piece of paper and put a copy somewhere where you will practically fall over it and when you do see it, say it then and there. You could say, "Jesus, I'm sorry I forgot awhile ago, but now I remember." If you didn't think of it until ten minutes ago or a half a day after you had blown your top over some annoyance; don't think, it's no use to say it now or it won't be any good to say it now. It will be good — good to help you form the good habit. So, say it right then.

Try to focus your mind on Jesus as you say it. He is in the room with you! Try to get that feeling. Again, if for some reason you forget the Morning Offering and think of it at three in the afternoon or nine-o-clock in the evening, say it then. The idea is to form the habit.

Don't despair and don't give up. It will grow on you more and more and it's a beautiful habit to have in your life. You are bringing Jesus right into your daily living. This is what we are striving for as Franciscans.

Notes

Notes

II St. Francis and His Early Companions

St. Francis' Early Life and Conversion

REFLECTIONS

My object in having this series of talks about St. Francis, is not only to take the shadowy figure of 800 years ago and SEE the flash and fire in his eyes; but also, to HEAR and grasp the whole message of his good news, so that we can bring that message into our present century and make it our way of life.

In these episodes, I am giving you the facts, but they are my interpretation and reflections of those facts. This is true also of anyone who has ever written anything about St. Francis. It's the only way to bring the facts to life and breathe the breath of life into them. Without that they are worthless. We need to walk right into the middle of his thoughts; into his heart and into his inner most feelings. We need to intrude into his privacy; to stick our noses into what he is doing at any given moment in the 13th Century when he was alive; and also, if we may use an exaggerated modern expression, drag him kicking and screaming into the presence of our hectic present day existence.

This is not far-fetched, because exaggerated expressions fit St. Francis to a "T" (Tau Cross). He was a master craftsman of exaggeration, both in truth and in deeds.

This story will take you from the gay troubadour that he was in his early years to the gathering of his first followers and the final decision to preach and follow the gospel as Christ wanted him to do.

Again, these things I am going to tell you about him will be colored by my own style and my own thoughts of what his life was all about. I will try to be factually accurate; but, he will look different to you than he does to me. You will be interpreting him with your own mind as I have with mine.

The questions I'm going to try to answer are: What was the most important thing in Francis' life? And why was he not lost in the obscurity of time, as most people are? The answer is: because of his conversion process.

I purposely said conversion process, because it didn't happen all of a sudden. He didn't kiss the leper and BANG, the light of conversion suffused him and he was a full-fledged saint.

No. It had its beginnings before that and it went on and on after that, agonizingly for him, more often than not.

FRANCIS' LIFE

I think it can be said to have begun when he was in prison for a year and he had much time to think.

But, before we go into that, let's take a look at what he was like BC — Before Conversion.

Picture this scene in Assisi in the early 13th Century — a narrow street at midnight — old houses, possibly in baroque architecture, and down the street comes a shouting, laughing, singing gang of youths. Their leader, though more slightly built than the rest, was the loudest of all. He was dressed in the showy costume of a minstrel or troubadour. His shoes were pointed, his socks a splash of many colors, his hooded tunic richly woven and also brightly colored, and his lute was slung carelessly in front of him.

This was Francis of Assisi, lover of a bulging purse and showy clothes; a first class show-off; a lover of *braggadocio* and a reckless spendthrift, who gloried in paying all the inflated tabs in the swanky taverns he and his friends frequented to wine and dine. His rich tenor voice often rose clear and beautiful, above the laughter and shouts of his companions, as he poured forth his gay troubadour ditties. He was inordinately gratified by the kudos of his parasitic companions who clung to his financial coattails and praised him for his wit.

This is the Francis that everyone knew before Christ entered his life — a life that would literally change the life of the Church.

REFLECTIONS

In this series we are going to try to discover not just factual details about the life of St. Francis, but much more his message and his spirit, so that we can bring that message and that spirit right into our lives as we seek to form ourselves as Franciscans.

First of all, we must not lose sight of the fact that, like Francis, we are a part of the material world, as well as the spiritual, and we must, every day, use things of the material world to sustain our existence. But, although we have this need for worldly things, we should always keep in mind that we must maintain a detached attitude towards them, not owning them or being owned by them, but recognizing and acknowledging that they are gifts from God for our use.

FRANCIS' LIFE

We said before that Francis' conversion process began early in his life and was encouraged by his year of imprisonment. So, let's talk about his imprisonment. How did it come about?

There was an age-old enmity between the citizens of Assisi, of which Francis was a native son, and the citizens of Perguia. In fact, to this day, animosity still exists between them.

Francis was a fiery, restless youth, always ready to fly off in behalf of some cause or another. Thus, when those of Assisi prepared to march into what they considered a just cause against the Perugians; Francis, like a tail-wagging puppy, was right at their heels, panting and barking excitedly, gleefully happy to be allowed to go with them.

Well, that didn't last very long, because very soon he and his fellow Perugians were ignominiously defeated at Ponte Giovanni and taken prisoner. Our eager little puppy now had his tail between his legs as he was marched off with the rest of them, over the old bridge and up into the walled city of Perugia.

His spirits soon revived however, and because of his gay, audacious manner, and his fine clothes, the jailers thought he was highborn like the nobles and knights, and they threw him into prison with them.

All during this year of imprisonment he was his usual gay, carefree self. But at the same time he had much time on his hands, and he did a great deal of thinking about himself, about his life, and where he was going and what he was going to do.

He was a good morale builder for the others because he was so jolly and lighthearted. He sang a great deal, and as we said, he loved to sing, and sing he did for his own and his companion's amusement.

REFLECTIONS

Take a minute and picture him in that dank, dark prison, sometimes sitting alone and lost in thought. Other times, an impish grin on his face, he deliberately intruded into the awareness of his fellow prisoners with his swaggering antics. Annoyed at first, they watched him and they saw his slim, slight figure pirouette before them in an exaggerated dance. If the twist had been in vogue at that time I'm sure he would have been doing the twist, and often, in pantomime. He would accompany himself by playing an imaginary fiddle, pretended to hold under his chin with one hand while with another he sawed away with an imaginary bow.

If you look you might see, reluctant at first, then with all-out delight, the smiles break over the faces of at least some of his companions. This sort of entertainment they liked. It was a joy and a breath of the freedom they had lost. They welcomed it and encouraged him, although he didn't need much encouragement. He was a born show-off and actor; an artist; a poet; a mystic and a lover — above all else, a lover. The true lover in him was dormant at this time, waiting ...

No one ever loved the way Francis loved — his love for Jesus was all out, toe to head, inside and out — all the way. And, the great love that was to flame up and consume him later was Jesus Christ crucified — it was to possess him, shake him and tear him from his roots and foundation. It would wrap him up and lock him in, never to be freed again. Such was his love for his Lord and Master, Jesus the Incarnate God. But wait, we're getting ahead of ourselves.

FRANCIS' LIFE

During his year's imprisonment his joyful manner both cheered and annoyed his companions. "How in the world," they complained, "can you be so cheerful in this dismal place?" His answer was a shrug and with a sudden twinge and a little frown, he became silent. He was realizing that he, himself, didn't know the answer to that question.

Why was he happy, when the others were so gloomy? He really didn't know. It was something inside him that had to come out.

"You must be out of your head," they told him. But he only answered gaily, and mysteriously, "Why shouldn't I be jolly? One day the whole world will bow down to me."

REFLECTIONS

He was right, of course, but not the way he was thinking right then in his carefree head. He was taking the wrong meaning as he did so often then and later. He was a starry-eyed boy in love with himself and he was thinking in terms of being a great hero, a crusader, a brave soldier glorious in battle.

All the while there was stirring inside him a smoldering mystery that was kindling a fire that later was to spill out like an erupting volcano — the fire of God's love and compassion.

Now he was unaware of what was at work inside him because he had not yet made the journey into himself where the real Francis was.

What significance does this have for us today?

It is what we, too, now need to do. We need to make this journey into ourselves, right down into our roots, to find the real "me" hidden inside, to fire it up and make it spill its compassion and understanding and brotherly love; to send it, not like destructive lava; but, like a softly illuminating candle flame into the market places of the world. This is the spirit of St. Francis moving in "me" that I am discovering in this *metanoia*, which I am working on and which is making me reach outside myself to embrace my brothers and sisters wherever I may find them.

FRANCIS' LIFE

One final thought about his year in prison. There was a young nobleman who was very shy, a wallflower type of person, who was lonely and who was looked down upon and ridiculed by the others. Francis took him under his protective wing. Francis was ever a champion of the lowly and oppressed, the weak ones of the world. He related to this shy person and drew him out of himself so that before too long the others, though perhaps grudgingly, began to accept him.

REFLECTIONS

Francis' compassion was as big as the whole wide world because he embraced the whole wide world and everybody and everything. This world was to him straight from God, created by God, who was and who is and who ever will be — LOVE.

FRANCIS' LIFE

Now we see Francis just emerging from his year of imprisonment. He is sickly, some think from malaria, others tuberculosis. He is quieter. He is, and always will be seen as a strange combination of gaiety and austerity — a man of childlike simplicity with a passion for perfection.

His whole conversion process carried him closer and closer to being a reflection of Jesus Christ, and in the last phase of his life it locked him hand and hand with the Suffering Servant, Jesus on the Cross.

Francis, too, was a man of sorrows and full of contrasts. He praised the sun and the moon and the stars, yet he often went away from these brothers and sisters of light into the gloom and mold of a darkened cave.

After his year of imprisonment, things didn't seem the same to him and was often and strangely depressed. He would return to the company of his old carefree friends, but they bored him. He found their actions not to his liking. His old way of living had gone flat — the champagne had lost its fizz.

Once, during this time of depression, he met a very poorly clad knight, and Francis impulsively exchanged his rich garments for the poor garment of the knight, while all the time thinking with longing, of becoming a great knight. The idea became an obsession with him, so much so that he had a dream about it one night. He saw a great palace; the walls were covered with glittering shields and bucklers and spears and helmets and many trophies of battle. Francis' dreaming eyes widened greedily. His arms reached out, wanting to gather them all in at one time. Oh, the wonder of them, he thought. Whose were they?

But even as the question flashed into his head an answer came, spoken out loud, in a very distinct voice. "They are yours, Francis."

"Glory be to God," he cried and in a rush of joy he was wide-awake and out of bed. Joy! Joy! This was for him! He would be a knight. Didn't this dream prove it?

Off he rushed with coat tails flying, riding off down the road toward Apulia. He would join the army of Walter of Brienne, who was a great knight leading his army in a crusade for Pope Innocent III.

He hadn't gone very far before he felt ill. He was annoyed. What was the matter with him? He was light-headed. He pulled up at an inn at Spoleto and headed straight for bed, and lay there wondering, fearful and dizzy.

Towards morning, half asleep, he suddenly heard that voice again and it sounded reproachful. "Francis, is it better to serve the master or the servant?" Francis sat up with a jerk. He could see no one; yet, there was the voice. "Oh Lord," he groaned, "What do you want of me?" "Return home," the voice urged him, "and wait there. I will tell you what I want you to do."

Instantly his spirits sank like a ball of lead. His elation of the day before flew right out the window. With dragging steps he left the inn. Reluctantly he turned his horse's head back towards Assisi.

His freeloading friends gathered around him. But he couldn't abide them any more. They were shallow, irresponsible and silly.

REFLECTIONS

Francis was restless. He withdrew and turned more and more to solitude. He prayed in secret; but didn't know it at the time he was beginning his journey into himself, his own personal *metanoia*, his root conversion.

FRANCIS' LIFE

Francis would spend his time in a cave in a mountain retreat and when he came down from his retreat, he would seek not his old friends, but the poor and became more kindly towards them. He was still dressing in the rich clothing his father gave him; but now, he would insist on having sewn in with the rich cloth some cloth of very poor quality. At that time it was a pattern in his life — reaching for his highest goal while wallowing in the depths.

He began to take an interest in old churches and their poor priests. He helped them financially with his father's money, much to the disappointment of his father.

In his restlessness, he went on a pilgrimage to the tomb of St. Peter. He saw many beggars standing outside the great church, and on an impulse he approached one of the most ragged beggars and struck up a conversation with him.

"Will you exchange your clothes for mine?" he asked.

The beggar's eyes popped. He stared at Francis' fine clothes, then down at his own rags.

"You've got to be kidding!" he said.

But Francis wasn't kidding. It took some persuasion to convince the poor man; but, before long, there was Francis standing outside of St. Peter's amidst the beggars — he, the most ragged of them all. He fingered the coarse, ragged garment he was wearing.

"Me," he marveled. "This is me in these rags!" Suddenly he grinned. He was enjoying himself immensely.

Back home he kept so aloof from his old friends that they were puzzled.

"You must be in love," they taunted him. That comment lit up his face with a smile.

"Yes," he agreed eagerly. "I am in love." I am going to marry the most beautiful lady anyone has ever seen."

They hooted with laughter. They didn't know he was referring to his Lady Poverty.

One friend often accompanied him when he withdrew into one of his mountain caves. This was a young man about his own age, whose name is not known. His friend would wait outside the cave while he went in alone to pray. His friend must have been a remarkably patient and understanding person to wait long hours outside for Francis.

These excursions took them to Mt. Subasio. Here Francis was beginning to find a priceless treasure, a growing and living awareness of Jesus.

But these were difficult times, this journey into himself. It was rugged, mysterious, fearful, arduous and agonizing. He regretted deeply his wasted life up to then and was uncertain of his future.

"God," he agonized. "You got me into this. You dragged me back from Walter of Brienne's crusade. Why? What do you want of me? You told me you would let me know what you wanted. Why aren't you telling me?"

He prayed in a sweat — his own private Gethsemane. He had a downright fear of the future and what was in store for him. Where was he headed? He was at loose ends, going nowhere. "God, you've got to help me," he cried.

God did, of course, in His own good time. God, he found out, would not be stampeded into action. He would find out that God goes at His own pace.

One day in the cave he was deep in prayer when something caught his eye, and he looked up in sheer astonishment. There, before him, life sized and alive, was Christ hanging in agony on the cross! Christ's eyes seemed to burn right into Francis. Christ's lips were drawn back from His teeth in terrible pain. His whole body was a picture of excruciating agony. Francis suddenly felt like a candle too close to a fire; his muscles, he was sure, were melting. Then the vision was gone.

For a long time Francis remained rooted to the spot; then he fell on his knees, rocking back and forth, his head hidden in his hands, moaning and weeping.

"I now know," he gasped, "I know what you want me to do. You are telling me I must deny myself, take up my cross and follow you."

In a daze he went forth from the cave and was never again the same. Christ crucified had branded Himself on his heart.

One day he was riding, deep in thought, through the countryside and not paying too much attention to where he was going. Suddenly he found himself near the forbidden area of the lepers. He saw a leper not far away and he shrank back. He was so close to the frightful figure he began to tremble with dread and abhorrence. He wanted to turn his horse and gallop away, but something was holding him there, and all at once there leaped into his mind again those words: "Take up your cross and follow me." Was this what that meant — this leper?

With a bound he was off his horse and striding towards the shrinking figure. He held out a handful of coins to the leper. Greedily a misshapen hand darted out and took the money. But Francis didn't stop at that. He put both arms around the loathsome figure and embraced him. He pressed his cheek against his and saw tears spring from the leper's sunken eyes.

Then he turned away, leaped back on his horse, and started off. He wasn't trembling any more and felt very odd. He looked back over his shoulder and gasped with incredulity. Where was the leper? Where he had stood there was no one. Francis was completely alone.

"Oh my God," he thought.

He felt such a rush of emotion that he reeled in his saddle. "God," he prayed. "Oh my good God."

He sat quite still for a while. Then a feeling of elation swept over him. He laughed. He felt lighthearted as a bird in flight. He felt he, himself, had wings. He could fly. He could fly. He could fly!

He burst into song and urged his horse into a gallop and down the road he sped. "O glory be to God," he sang. (Ruth has a slightly different version of this story in her article, "Franciscan Commitment," page 30).

In the spirit and awe of God he went on to his cave to pray, and then, in a high movement of spiritual closeness to God, a most disturbing thing happened to him.

Into the solitude of his cave came the devil himself. Francis saw him, stared at him and then shrank from him. He shivered and felt like screaming. The devil spoke to him. "Remember that hideous hunchbacked derelict in town?" The devil's voice was raspy and disjointed. It grated on Francis' ears and made his blood run cold. The devil said to him, "I will make you just like him if you don't stop this stupid way you are going." But quickly and urgently another voice inside Francis said, "Don't pay any attention to him. Believe in Me. BELIEVE IN ME!"

He knelt and prayed. He felt great sorrow for his past life and his wasted time. He thought of Jesus hanging on the cross and how Jesus came alive in his life — the love of Jesus, greater than anything he had ever imagined.

And thus was his conversion process solidifying, embedding its roots in the deepest recesses of his being. His *metanoia* was moving along in high gear.

REFLECTIONS

We have reached the point in Francis' conversion where Jesus has become the real person in his life — Jesus crucified.

FRANCIS' LIFE

About this time in his life we have the San Damiano incident. Francis was on his way somewhere when he passed a dilapidated church. He was so deep in thought that he almost walked by it before he noticed it was a church (he never passed by a church without popping in). He backtracked to the front door and entered. He looked around and saw that the interior of the church was in sad shape. The roof was so badly caved in, in some places, that he could see the sky through it. Stones and rubble were scattered on the floor beneath the crumbling walls.

He shook his head and saddened him profoundly. He fell on his knees and started to pray. He stared at a large crucifix that was over the altar. It was different from any crucifix he had seen before; actually, it was a Byzantine crucifix (see page 89). The Christ figure was surrounded by other figures of saints.

Francis raised his eyes to those of Christ. Going through his head was the starkly and realistic vision of the living Christ on the cross. His eyes seem to be fixed on those on the crucifix and tears sprang into his eyes. Half blinded with tears he stared dumbfounded at the crucifix. He blinked away the tears and did a double take. Yes! He did see the lips of Christ moving. They were uttering words and the words were coming out quite audibly.

"Francis, repair my church which, as you see, is falling into ruin."

Francis was stunned. He got to his feet and walked distractedly about the church, stopping to look at the worst places of disrepair. It certainly was falling into ruin, he thought to himself.

He went back to the crucifix and stood gazing at it. It was lifeless now, just an inanimate cross with an inanimate figure on it. He was puzzled. Had he been mistaken? Had he imagined he heard it speak? No! He was sure he had seen the lips move and heard the words.

"Glory be to God," he cried in a rapture. "This is what my Lord told me to wait for. This is what He wants me to do." He experienced a great surge of joy. Without further ado, he rushedd out of the church and began to beg, borrow, or let us say it mildly, "steal," some of the materials — the stones, mortar, and boards, he needed to repair the church. He worked until the sweat rolled off him. From time to time a few other youths, attracted by his enthusiasm, help him.

REFLECTIONS

He went into this new phase of his conversion on the run. He was always running, even in his latter years, running towards the outstretched arms of his Savior.

Now, in throwing himself headlong into repairing the church of San Damiano, he had something concrete to fasten onto; something the Christ on the crucifix had told him to do.

FRANCIS' LIFE

He gave the poor priest who came to live there a handful of money and asked him to use it to buy oil to keep the lamp always burning before the crucifix.

Repairing the church, he knew would take some doing. What to do? He needed money. He hadn't yet reached the phase in his conversion where he despised money.

He paced back and forth, his hands clasped behind his back. Suddenly a thought came into his mind and he snapped his fingers. He had it! He was the indulged son of a rich father, wasn't he? So he thought he would take a few bales of his father's cloth and sell them.

He mounted one of his father's finest horses and off he rode to the city of Foligno and there, without thinking of the consequences, he sold not only the cloth, but the horse as well.

Soon, back in San Damiano he eagerly held out the money to the poor priest. The priest was taken aback. "Oh no," the priest protested. But Francis insisted that he take the money. "You need it," he said, "for repairs. I will help you and work here myself. I thought," he went on hopefully, "I could live here with you. Please let me live here."

Aware that he knew how Francis got the money the priest sighed and said, "You may live here, but I cannot take the money. It belongs to your father. You should not have taken the cloth and the horse. It was wrong."

He put the purse back in Francis' hand and kindly, but firmly, closed the young man's fingers about it.

Francis looked with distaste at the money. All of a sudden he hated it, what was it to him? He didn't want any part of it and with a contemptuous gesture he hurled it onto a window sill.

His father, Pietro Bernardone, soon got wind of what Francis had done. In a rage he charged down upon the little church and the poor old priest.

"Where's my son," his father demanded.

But, that was the question, where was Francis?

Anticipating his father's anger, Francis had turned chicken and was hiding in a little cave not far away.

His father stormed around for a while; but, unable to find him, he gave way to two emotions, alternately he was beside himself with rage, then overwhelmed with genuine grief. He was unable to understand how this son of his, on whom he had lavished his affection and his goods, could have done such a complete about face as to become this weirdo that the whole town of Assisi was laughing at. His father hung his head in shame.

Francis, in hiding, was praying intensely and beseeched God to help him. After a time, peace began to come over him and he began to reproach himself for being a coward.

With that thought, he rose up, out of his hiding place and strode with determination down the road towards Assisi.

The Assisians looked upon Francis at that time as a rich, pleasure-loving, playboy-jongleur, and impeccable dresser. Now, here he came, looking anything but impeccable. He was disheveled, wild in appearance, downright dirty and a perfect picture of a modern day hippie at his sloppiest worst.

The townsfolk thought he had gone bananas. They didn't hesitate to ridicule him. They even threw stones and mud at him.

His father hastened to meet him. This was no Gospel father going out to meet his prodigal son. This was a red-hot parent, after his maddening, crazy, mixed-up son.

He seized Francis, dragged him into the house, and beat him, not sparing the rod, in true Old Testament fashion. Then he threw him, shaken and bruised into his dark cellar, in chains.

REFLECTIONS

You see how often Francis goes from light into darkness, from freedom into a dark cellar. It was like before when he went into that dark, dank prison. He often went from sunlight into musty caves and from open decisive action to the darkness and uncertainty of an unknown future. There are times when we experience the same things.

FRANCIS' LIFE

Pietro beat him again and again, trying, to make him see reason, but it was to no avail.

About this time Pietro had to go out of town. Francis' mother, through all this, was terribly grieved, the situation tormented her. She couldn't stand having him chained in the dark cellar. After Pietro took off, she pleaded with him to change, but he would not. He could not, he told her. So, she set him free anyway. She was afraid to the point of trembling and of the consequences, but still set him free.

Actually, according to civil law of that time, Francis, for his rebellious actions, was subject to the punishment of being shunned by everyone; being banished altogether from the region, or of being imprisoned.

But when his father returned and confronted him with this, he coolly informed his father that he was no longer under civil authority because, at the time his father had seized him, he had been living with the poor priest at San Damiano. He, therefore, was subject to the clause in Pope Innocent III's recent bull, which gave the bishop judiciary power over clerics and people on church property. So, Pietro promptly took him to the bishop.

On April 16, 1207. Bishop Guida, who later became a friend and spiritual advisor to Francis, had a hearing in the public square, which gathered quite a crowd.

"Francis," the bishop said, "first of all you have to return your father's money to him."

"No problem," Francis replied. "Not only will I give back the money, but also my clothes."

He threw the money at his father's feet; a rude act indeed, then stripped himself naked and hurled his clothing, too, at his father. He threw back his head and cried out to heaven, "I have nothing left belonging to Pietro Bernadone. From now on I shall say, 'Our Father who art in Heaven.' He, from now on, is my only Father."

Actually, it has been said, he had one garment remaining on him, a hair shirt.

One account of the episode says: His father rose up, burning with grief and anger, and gathered up the garments and the money and carried them home. And with them, he carried inside himself a father's broken heart. It wasn't easy to be the father of Francis.

Shocked, no doubt, by this sudden stripping act, the bishop rushed to Francis and covered him with his own mantle. He sent a servant to fetch something for Francis to put on. The servant came back with an old, warn-out farmer's tunic and Francis put it on. Later, on the front of the tunic, he drew in white chalk a crusader's cross. He was now embarked on his own private crusade and thus was born the "habit" of the Franciscans and a new man of God, on his way to unbelievable spiritual heights and honor.

Now, Francis entered into a new life and became a different sort of knight than what he had dreamed of being.

One day he was going along minding his own business he was roughly beset on by robbers. It was obvious they could not have hoped to get anything of value from him, because he was in much worse shape than they were. He looked like something left out in the rain then brought in and dried out.

He was not afraid of the robbers, at least he pretended not to be. He looked them squarely in the eye and declared with an audacious swagger, his ragged tunic flapping about his bare legs, "I am the herald of a great King." Well that got them! They laughed uproariously and clapped each other on the back.

"Now I've heard everything!" One of them yelled. He was a huge fellow, and towered over Francis. He was rough and bearded. He minced about mockingly and mimicked Francis. "I am the herald of a great king," he said.

Then, with a sudden swoop, he seized Francis, held him high in the air, then dragged him like an empty sack squarely into a ditch filled with dirty, melting snow. He bent over Francis and pushed his face into the snow. Francis came up gasping. Down went his face again and then a third time. The snow was cold and he was half drowned.

Finally, after sneezing, coughing and spitting out dirty snow, he got to his feet. He shook himself off, looked up at his tormentors and smiled disarmingly, "Good morning good people," he said graciously. His smile broadened. It was genuinely mirthful and friendly; they stared at him, baffled.

"I don't believe this," one of them muttered. "This guy can't be for real."

He turned away, shaking his head and the others followed him. Francis heard one of them mutter, "Cuckoo!"

Francis laughed aloud.

"Cuckoo, cuckoo," he repeated like a clock measuring the hours. "Was my Lord Jesus cuckoo, too?"

Later he trudged on up Mt. Subasio and came to a place of cloistered monks and stopped at the front door. He reached out his hand, to knock, then drew it back. "Will they let me in?" he wondered. "Well here goes," he thought, and he knocked on the door.

The door flew open and he found himself confronted by a big monk who was glaring at him like a bear reared up on his hind legs. Francis gulped.

"Well, what do you want," the monk demanded.

"May I ... that is, I thought …"

Francis found himself stammering. "Don't be a jerk," he told himself. "Are you a man or a mouse?"

"May I come in" he said, stoutly. "I hoped you might let me stay here for awhile." The monk's eyes were boring holes in him. After what seemed to Francis an interminable time, the monk stepped back and motioned him to come in. He was still eyeing Francis with suspicion. "If you stay a while," he said, "you will have to work." Francis did work and oh, how he worked — hard menial jobs and cheerfully singing as he worked.

He emptied slop pails, scrubbed floors, washed dirty clothes and pots and pans, and all the while he sang.

From time to time he caught their questioning looks at him. "Cuckoo," he said under his breath. "That's me, a Cuckoo." He laughed at his own joke. Humbly he accepted the thin broth they gave him to eat, but there came a time when his ragged tunic was no longer fit to hang on his skinny body. He asked them timidly, "Do you have some old thing I could have to replace this?" as he touched his ragged garment. They ignored his request.

They turned against him then, if it can be said they ever had turned towards him. As a matter of fact, some time later when his sanctity had become well known to all about the countryside, that same monk came to him, and, on his knees, begged his forgiveness. Still they turned him out.

The big door slammed behind him, and here he was again outside, alone and nowhere to go. He went to Gubbio and there he found an old friend who gave him a cast-off garment, which he accepted gladly. He took up residence in a leper colony and stayed there as their servant, like Jesus Christ. He tenderly washed their feet, washed their sores, and cleaned their ulcers. He looked compassionately at their rotting flesh and thought, with a rueful smile, of the times in Assisi when he had stood far off and held his nose and shuddered at the sight of their foul physical condition. Now, he rose his eyes heavenward and sighed, "How could I have been like that?" he wondered. It made him sad to think of it.

"Forgive me, my Lord," he begged. "Help me to learn how to console, to understand, to forgive, and to love as you do. Make me an instrument of your blessed way."

The leper colony was not far from San Damiano and he remembered Christ's command to him to rebuild His church. Francis left the leper colony and it was then that he threw himself heart and soul into the task. He had no resources whatever now and had to work with his bare hands. His physical strength sometimes was unequal to the task; but, his determination was boundless.

When he needed to, he begged and exhorted those around him. And, of course, he prayed. The very seeming impossibility of accomplishment drew a few other youths to help him. Eventually, sweating and almost exhausted, with his eyes bright with triumph, he stood before that little church and saw it restored. "This is all for the love of God," he cried.

REFLECTIONS

Francis, when he needed to, begged, and when he begged he also prayed. There is an important message here for us Secular Franciscans.

The message is not that we should go from door to door with an empty bowl and receive the scraps that people drop into it, but that we should take this as an example of how not to give alms. We should not give useless, worn out, spoiled things — things we want to get rid of in the name of charity.

It is also a lesson for us with regard to the things we buy for ourselves. We should be satisfied with less, we do not have to have the best of all things.

Francis' piety was robust. He refused to be pampered like a spoiled child. And, that is another lesson for us Franciscans. Aren't we like spoiled children much of the time? We don't like this, and we don't like that. Isn't it time we started being adult Christians? Are we striving to form ourselves as Franciscans?

We should ask ourselves these questions often in our quest for forming our way of St. Francis. His way is the Gospel way — the way of Jesus.

"When I was a child I spoke like a child. But when I became a man I put off the things of a child and became a man." All the things Francis had done up to now testify to this and his progressive conversion — his putting on the beggar's garments in front of St. Peters; his exchanging his fine garments for those of a poor knight; his kissing the leper; his selling of his father's cloth and horse to get money for the church (a wrong act but a right motive); his stripping himself naked; his tending the ulcerated flesh of a leper and now his begging from door to door, attest to this.

FRANCIS' LIFE

Francis went about the city begging oil to keep the lamp before the crucifix burning in San Damiano's. All this begging was very painful for him because he still had his pride and still could be embarrassed.

One day when he went begging for oil he hesitated at a house where men were gambling. He was ashamed to go in and started to walk past the house, then he stopped. "No," he told himself, "I must not be ashamed to beg oil for God." His whole being shrunk back, rebelling against appearing like a fool in front of those sophisticated men.

Once more he walked away; but, with a sudden resolution he whirled and strode into their presence.

"I'm a sinner," he blurted, thumping his chest. "Take a look at me, I was too proud just now to come in here and beg alms for God's church, but now I'm begging for the love of God." They looked at the little beggar, half amused, half sympathetic and gave him some oil.

And, he got something else. He got a big "A" on his report card for Humility — big, beautiful, sincere, real, down deep, Christ-centered HUMILITY.

During this time when he was living at the little church of San Damiano, he repaired the little church of St. Mary of the Angels. It was said that angels often visited the little church. That is probably why it was known as St. Mary of the Angels or, maybe he just gave it that name. We know he loved the church very dearly, so much so that he made it the mother church of his three

Orders.

He asked to be carried to it when he was near death. And it was at this beloved little portiuncula, this little portion of ground that he died, flat on his back, lying at his request, on the bare earth.

In rebuilding these churches he did not have in mind simply to restore the edifices, but much more, to provide a suitable reverential place for the celebration of the Sacrifice of the Mass and the Holy Eucharist.

Out of this restoration of churches came one of his well known prayers:

"We adore you, most holy Lord Jesus Christ,
Here and in all the churches throughout
the whole world, and we bless you,
because by your most holy cross
You have redeemed the world."

It was in this little church, St. Mary of the Angels, that he received the final impetus in his conversion process. It set him on his Gospel way to draw followers, few at first, then an avalanche of them down through the centuries.

REFLECTIONS

In talking about St. Francis, we are going into his transition from his conversion process into the evolution of his three Orders.

What he was doing now in his preaching was the repair of Christ's Church from within that Christ had advocated from the crucifix in the San Damiano Church. Francis now was all-afire to bring Christ strongly back into His Church.

In his preaching he was making Christ come alive in the mind and hearts of those who followed him. It was not just his eloquent preaching, though, that drew followers to him, albeit he was a forceful and inspiring speaker, it was his zeal for Christ electrifying those that heard him. But, even louder than his words was the message of his example. These two things together were an irresistible force that drew many souls to him along his Gospel way.

Francis' three Orders mushroomed from then on.

He had had no idea at all at the outset of his conversion of starting any religious order. He was engaged simply in bringing about his own *metanoia*.

His reforming of himself snowballed into reformation of Christ's Church from within, unlike the reformers who came after him, who left the church altogether and sought reformation by starting their own new religious movements. How did the later reformers think they could reform Christ's

Church by deserting it? Only by staying within the Church, as Francis did, could it be reformed.

We Franciscans need this reformation within ourselves — our own personal *metanoia*.

A happy result of our reforming ourselves is that in doing so, we too are making our church and the world a better place.

There was a story to illustrate this point: A man was trying to read his newspaper one evening, but his little boy kept interrupting him.

In exasperation, the father ripped a page from a geography book showing a map of the world and tore it into pieces. He gave the pieces to the boy and said, "There, put that together like a jig-saw puzzle." He thought this would keep the boy busy for a good long time. But soon the boy was back with it all together.

"How in the world did you do it so fast?" the father asked in astonishment.

"It was easy," the boy stated matter-of-factly. "There was the picture of a man on the other side. I knew if I got the man right I would get the world right."

That is what Francis did. He got the man right first.

Now, back to our story about Francis.

FRANCIS' LIFE

His first follower was a man of Assisi, simple and good of which nothing is told; the second was Bernard of Quintavalle and the third was Dr. Peter of Catanii.

Peter was a learned man, a lay canon at the Cathedral, a doctor of laws. He and Bernard were well acquainted and he, too, had been watching Francis for some time. Now, when he saw Bernard dispossessing himself of his worldly goods to join Francis, he was eager to do likewise. "This is for me, too," he told himself, and lost no time in joining them. Peter sold his possessions, although quite well-to-do, but not in the category of Bernard, who had been ranked among Assisi's highest born and wealthiest citizens. Both these men put on the habit Francis had designed.

The three of them now took up residence at Rivo Torto (as far as I know, where Rivo Torto is, is unknown). What is known is that these early brothers lived in an abandoned hovel at a place called by that name, Rivo Torto, or Twisted Stream, somewhere on the plain near Assisi.

There is a big church on the high road to Foligno that some claim covers the hovel, but many writers say it is almost 2 miles farther up the road, where there are two ancient chapels.

One author, Ernest Raymond, when he was in that area in the 1930's said an old woman got a key for him and unlocked the door of one of these ancient chapels, the one known as San Rufino Chapel.

This author says the yard about the chapel was occupied by a mother hen who was fussily clucking and ruffling her feathers amid her brood of chicks, and when he stepped through the now open door, mama hen, still fussily talking, herded her chicks right alongside him into the chapel. They, the author and the chickens, all looked about with lively interest. What they saw was a dusty, oblong room with a stone altar. Dried remnants of potatoes and tomatoes; barrels of flour, and casks of wine were scattered all over the floor, with onions on the altar step.

Somewhere in the area of this little chapel was that tiny hovel where Francis lived with his first brothers (he never referred to them as his followers, they were his brothers).

This little hut was so small they were crowded like peas in a pod, so Francis marked off, with white chalk, little spaces, one for each brother and that was where each brother had to *live.*

This was one of the most joyful and peaceful periods of their lives. Together, this little band of brothers grew to love one another with a true Christ-like love.

The fourth one to follow Francis was Giles. Giles was a sturdy youth who came popping out of the woods one day and sought to join them. He was a farmer's son — a plough boy.

They made room for him and was with them several days and still in his lay clothes when a poor man happened in and asked for alms. Francis looked at the poor man, then at Giles. "Brother Giles," he said, "give this poor man your cloak." Francis watched him narrowly. Since Giles had just wandered in, Francis had no idea what his reaction would be to this suggestion. But he didn't need to wonder long because the words were no sooner out of his mouth than Giles stripped off his cloak and with a bow and a broad smile, handed it to the beggar. Francis clapped his hands together, delighted. "Brother Giles, you're one of us!" he exclaimed.

And forthwith he clothed the happy young man with the crude habit and cord of the other friars.

So now there were four of them crowded into the little hovel that really wasn't much better than a chicken coop. So Francis got out his chalk again and marked off another small section for Giles.

Giles was a simple and upright young man, God-loving and a perfect example of obedience. He was strong and a good worker, not shunning hard manual labor at which he went at cheerfully. He also was a man who, like Francis, liked solitary times when he became rapt in deep and holy contemplation. It was said he lived to a very old age.

There is an interesting story told about Brother Giles.

King Louis of France was on a pilgrimage, traveling incognito. He had heard a lot about the saintliness of brother Giles and the King had set his heart on meeting him.

He had heard that Giles was in Perugia, so the King, disguised as an ordinary pilgrim, went to the "little place" in Perugia where Giles and a number of the friars, were staying. The brothers called the small huts where they lived a "little place."

The porter, not knowing who the king was, brought him to Giles. Giles was given a spiritual insight, which enabled him, instantly, to see through the king's disguise.

Happily and marveling at the sight of the king, Giles ran to meet the king and they literally ran into each other's arms, each embracing the other as though they were friends of long standing. They remained clasped together like that for a long time, wordlessly locked heart to heart. Then, still without a word, they parted and the king and his companions rode off.

After he had gone, Giles excitedly told the others who the visitor was. They looked at him dumbfounded. They reproached him. "Why didn't you speak to him, show him more respect." Giles shook his head, smiling, his eyes bright with joy. "We didn't need to speak," he assured them. "In that embrace the light of divine wisdom revealed his heart to me and mine to him. And so, by God's grace, we looked into each other's heart and our thoughts to each other WE HEARD without sound, better than if we had spoken out loud."

He was quiet for a moment, happily reliving the encounter, then went on. "The defect of human language cannot clearly express the secret mysteries of God and could not have consoled us. But you should know that the King departed greatly consoled."

The king, as we know, is the Patron of our Third Order and has long been listed among its canonized saints.

Soon they were no longer four followers, because they were joined by, Sabbatino, Morico, John of Capella and "Philip the Long," so called because he was very tall. It was said of Philip that he was touched on the lips by an angel with a burning coal, like Isaiah. He was well versed in Holy Scripture and understood it so well he was looked to for interpretations even though he had not studied. He was an eloquent speaker.

Then they were joined in uncertain order by another John, this one of Costanzo; Bernardo Vigilanta; Barbaro; and Angelo Tancredi, who rounded out the first known twelve brothers, according to some authors. Other authors vary in some of the names of the first twelve.

Not much is known about some of these men. One of them, John of Capella, later strayed into evil ways and ended by hanging himself like Judas, one of Christ's twelve apostles. Angelo Tancredi of Rieti was renowned for his courtesy and loyalty. More is known about him than some of the others. Angelo was a knight of position and wealth in the Vale of Rieti. He was young and full of youthful exuberance. His house was in a secluded spot, hidden behind a windowless building. It is still in use, so it is said, by a contemplative order of Franciscan nuns, probably Poor Clares.

Angelo became one of a group of four brothers who stayed very close to Francis all his life; almost, it has been said, like a body guard. After their deaths, Angelo, Masseo, Rufino, and Leo were buried in the same church with Francis in the middle and one on each side of him at the four corners, as though guarding him still. Leo, Rufino and Angelo were the authors of "The Legend of the Three Companions."

Another of the early friars was a priest named Sylvester. This priest had been approached a good while before Francis went begging stones to rebuild the little churches. Francis asked Sylvester for stones and Sylvester gave him some for a small fee.

When Bernard of Quintavalle and Francis were distributing Bernard's wealth to the poor, Sylvester got wind of it and went to them with his hand out.

"Ahem!" he began and touched Francis on the sleeve. Francis looked around at him. He saw Sylvester lick his lips with a greedy light in his eyes. Francis' own eyes narrowed and he waited for Sylvester to say something.

Sylvester cleared his throat again. He had the grace to be a bit embarrassed, but his greed held sway.

"I ... that is, you will remember that I gave you some stones to help rebuild the church? You didn't pay me very much for them you know!"

A little flush touched Francis' cheeks and he looked at Sylvester long and hard.

"We were giving this money to those we feel need it more than we do," Francis pointed out. "But since you feel you are one of them — here!" And he thrust a handful of coins into the priest's outstretched hand. Sylvester clutched it. Then with a tight-lipped smile, that was partly triumph, but also tinged with an inner uneasiness, he turned and strode away.

By the time he reached his home there was a stricken look in his eyes. He was remembering the look of hurt and sadness that had come over Francis' face as he took the money.

He didn't know that Francis had had an odd conviction, even as he looked at Sylvester's receding back, that, not only had he not seen the last of Sylvester, but that the time would come when he would see a halo about the priest's head.

And of course that is what happened. Sylvester is also listed among the canonized saints of the Franciscan Order.

It is said that, "when Sylvester went to bed that night he was already deeply repenting what he had done. That night, and for two more nights thereafter, he had a vision from God of Francis. From Francis' mouth came a gold cross. The top of the cross reached to Heaven while its arms seemed to extend from east to west to the ends of the earth."

As a result of the vision he was touched by the Lord and he disposed of all his property and gave it to the poor. He became a Friar Minor and he was often rapt in contemplation.

Sylvester was perhaps the first ordained priest to become a Friar Minor.

As an example of the high degree of sanctity, with which Francis later regarded him, there was the time when Francis was in mental turmoil because of his in-decision as to whether he should lead a strictly contemplative life, which he yearned for or like Christ's disciples, go out and preach. Something kept nagging at him to do the latter even though he so very much preferred the former. That something, of course, was God.

So, Francis sent one of the brothers with a message to Sylvester. "Tell him to pray intensely to God until he gets an answer to the question as to whether I am to live the life of a hermit, or go forth and preach the Gospel to the people." At the same time Francis sent another brother to St. Clare with the same urgent request.

Soon, the messengers came back to him and each gave him the reply received from God by Sylvester and Clare. The answers were identical. Both Clare and Father Sylvester said: "God has revealed to me that you, Francis, are not for yourself alone. You are for the entire world. You must go forth and spread the Gospel message among all the people."

Brother Rufino

My dear brothers and sisters, St. Francis could be stern as well as compassionate. During lent, a time of penance, a story from which I am about to tell you, brings out the beautiful simplicity, childlike qualities and desire for penance of St. Francis.

This story concerns Brother Rufino. Rufino was so absorbed in heavenly things that he hardly noticed anything that went on around him. He was not much of a preacher, so when St. Francis one day said to him, "I want you to go to a church in Assisi and preach to the people," Brother Rufino was taken aback and in a most humble way asked to be excused because he had no talent in that direction. St. Francis, in his impetuous way, instantly rebuked him and said sternly, "Since you did not obey me when I asked you, I now command you to go, and to go naked except for your underwear, and preach in some church in Assisi." Brother Rufino gulped and paled, but without a word he started off. On the way he was accosted buy jeering boys who tagged at his heels and cried out, "These brothers are so wrapped up in penance that they have gone crazy." Brother Rufino kept going straight into a church and up into the pulpit where he did indeed start to preach.

In the meantime, Francis, back at the monastery, was struck with remorse. "Here is this man of high noble birth," he accused himself, "whom you, a nobody, have sent off on this humiliating task. Now," he told himself sternly, "you can just go and do this same thing yourself that you made him do." He disrobed and called brother Leo, "I'd like you to accompany me."

Brother Leo stared at him, shook his head and hurried out of the room, calling back, "I'll be right with you." Soon he was back with a mysterious knapsack slung over his shoulder. Off they went and when they were trudging into Assisi they, too, were greeted with jeers and hoots of laughter.

St. Francis held his peace, but was humiliated. He, with a red faced Brother Leo trudging along beside him, hastened on into the church where Brother Rufino was preaching, and doing a creditable job of it.

Looking up at the pulpit, Francis stopped, aghast; there high above him in the pulpit was Brother Rufino looking for all the world like a great featherless bird.

"Is that the way I look?" Francis gasped with a quick glance down at his own nakedness. Shaking his head, he strode forward and joined Brother Rufino in the pulpit. He motioned Brother Rufino back, swallowing hard and cleared his throat loudly, which helped steady him. Quavering, he began to preach. Laughter came up at him. His voice grew louder. Soon it's beauty was going out like a great bell until it's sonorous tones filled the length and breadth of the church. The silly grins on the faces below began to fade. He preached eloquently, of poverty, humility, and penance. A hush fell over the assembly when he depicted Christ's humiliation, aloneness, and nakedness, as He hung on the Cross. Sobs shook many a hardened sinner and tears splashed down many a weather-beaten face. Gone was any vestige of contempt; in its place were sorrow, repentance, deep reverence, and a great swelling of conversion in the hearts of the people.

He finished and stepped back and Brother Leo hurried forward and opened his knapsack and out of it he took the two habits for the naked duo. Without a word he handed one to each and each man gratefully took the habit and put it on. Then, with sheepish grins all around, they left the church and marched homeward, not abjectly though; but, in triumph because their hearts were high in the glory of God and because they knew there were many people converted in Assisi that day. As a matter off fact, there were many who were so struck with the holiness of these men that they desired nothing better than the privilege of just touching their garments with the utmost reverence.

REFLECTIONS

A thought for us to take home might be to strip ourselves of the inner garment of pride and put on the inner garment that Christ is taking out of His knapsack and handing to each one of us. The garment is humility, which could lead to self-accusation, self-denial, repentance and heartfelt sorrow for even our venial sins and a firm resolution to *"go and sin no more."* In particular, to overcome the same old sins, confession after confession.

To the glory of our Lord Jesus Christ, Amen.

Brother Leo

I think we might look upon the relationship between St. Francis and Brother Leo in somewhat the same way as John, the Beloved Apostle, was to Christ.

Leo, of all the brothers, was the closest to Francis. He was an unimposing shy little priest, who was chosen by Francis as his confessor and spiritual counselor. He also served Francis as secretary. He was a skilled penman, artistically so. He was the chief of the authors who knew St. Francis intimately. He was one of the three companions who wrote the *"Legend of the Three Companions."* Francis called him his "Pecorello di Dio," the "Little Sheep of God." His writings, it has been said, were instrumental in preserving for posterity the message of St. Francis.

Leo, unlike his namesake, the four-legged brother lion, was gentle and mild; yet, he could on occasion, assume a fierce attitude in defense of St. Francis. He was, if we may make the comparison, Francis' faithful watchdog, happy just to be able to follow at his heels.

One day he and Francis were going from Perugia to Assisi, Leo walking ahead and Francis a few paces behind. It was snowing heavily and they were cold and poorly clad for such a long and rugged walk in a blizzard.

Francis called out to Leo, "O Brother Leo ..." Leo turned his head a bit to indicate he was listening; then began the famous teasing and challenging litany of what did "not" constitute perfect joy.

"The friars," Francis sang out, "could give great example of sanctity to all, but that would not be perfect joy."

Leo's breath was frosting the air as he listened expectantly for Francis to tell him what was perfect joy. But Francis was not ready yet.

"O Brother Leo, if the friars were great healers and even could raise the dead to life ..." This was It, Leo thought. But no, there was a silence.

"O brother Leo, if they had the knowledge of prophets, Francis called in his lilting voice.

Now, Leo thought. But, again Leo sighed, for that was not the answer. "O Brother Leo," came Francis' voice again, "if they were great preachers." And only silence followed this.

Leo clenched his fists. He was slowly going out of his mind waiting for the rest of the answer, as only silence lay between them.

Leo threw up his arms and whirled on Francis. "For God's sake, brother Francis," he cried, "tell me what IS perfect joy?

Francis' eyes were merry as he answered, "Why brother Leo, if we came to the Portiuncula, and the porter opened the door to our knock, and bellowed that he did not know us, and then came out and threw us face down in the snow and kicked us three or four times, then went back inside and slammed the door and locked it, leaving us outside, wet and shivering and not knowing what to do next; THAT would be perfect joy."

REFLECTIONS

In our formation process, from these tales of Francis and his early followers, we as his followers should ask ourselves, "What does this tell me?"

It tells me a few things about St. Francis: It shows his own patience in suffering ... his humility and his physical endurance. And, that there was a little imp of merriment inside him, a great sense of humor underlying his seriousness and sanctity and his great affection for Brother Leo, his pecorello, his "Little Sheep of God."

And it should tell all of us, not just that this is an interesting little anecdote about St. Francis, but inside of that, just as it was inside the parables of Jesus, there is a message.

What is the message? Ask yourself.

This is what we should think about when we read these things. This is what helps us in our ongoing formation as Franciscans.

I toss this out to you to take home with you. In the light of this message from Francis, what is perfect joy for you in your life? Think about it and meditate on it. Take a hand in your own formation as a Franciscan and a Catholic.

LEO'S LIFE

Leo was with Francis at La Verna at the time of Francis' Stigmata, and for a period preceding that event.

Francis had a great need for solitude at that time. He was in very poor health and had periods of despondency as well as anyone else. Some of the brothers were giving him a hard time.

So, he went to the quiet majesty of La Verna Mountain. He took with him a few of his "disciples" as did Jesus at Gethsemane. Leo, of course, was one of them.

Francis had a little cell apart from the rest where he could be alone. Only Leo was allowed to come near, to bring him a little bread and water now and then.

This went on for a few days; but even that was not the complete solitude

Francis craved, so he called Leo to him.

"Leo," he said, "stand in this doorway while I go up yonder and when I call to you, come to me.

He climbed up the mountain, turned and called, "Leo! Leo!"

Leo hurried to him.

"Go back, and I will call to you again," Francis said.

He climbed higher. This time when he called, "Leo, Leo," there was no answer. He was satisfied; he was truly alone.

He had the brothers build a bridge of logs across a narrow chasm and on the other side they built him a rough cell.

No one was to come near him again except Leo, who could come as far as the bridge only once during the day and once at night.

Francis forbade Leo to come at any other time and never beyond the bridge.

But one day when Leo came to the bridge and called to Francis, there was no answer. Puzzled, Leo hesitated, then crossed the bridge and looked into Francis' cell. It was empty. No doubt wondering if Francis was all right, since he was in poor health, he began quietly to search the woods. He came upon Francis kneeling, his face uplifted. A great shaft of fire was resting on his head. Leo heard Francis say, "Who art thou, O my most sweet God, and what am I, but a most vile worm and worthless servant ..."

Very quietly Leo withdrew and was stealing away when Francis heard the rustling of leaves.

Francis called to him to stop him in his tracks. Leo stopped, trembling with dread that Francis would be angry with him and wouldn't want him for his companion any longer.

"Why have you done this, little sheep?" Francis asked him.

Leo hung his head. He was overwhelmed with remorse, but Francis was kind to him and said, "Know, brother Little Sheep, that when I said those words you heard, there was shown to me in my soul two lights, one of the understanding of myself and the other of the knowledge of the Creator. Now go, and don't watch me any more."

This took place a few days before the imposition of the stigmata on his hands and feet and side.

Leo was with Francis when he died as he was with St. Clare when she died. When Leo died, an old man in 1271, his eyes were closed by Francis' very good friend, the Lady Giacoma Settisoli, whom Francis called Brother Jacopa. She died shortly after him and was buried beneath St. Francis' tomb in the Basilica of St. Francis in Assisi. Leo is one of the four who are buried at the four corners of St. Francis tomb in that Basilica.

REFLECTIONS
This ends my thoughts and reflections on the early life and conversion of St. Francis. My hope is that those who read about his life will want to follow his way and truly follow the Way of the Gospel.

Notes

*"Francis greeted them and
explained the word of God
in a loud voice,
'as clear as a bugle.'"*

The First Chapter of Mats

St. Francis called a General Chapter to meet on the plain of St. Mary of the Angels. There were over 5000 who attended that first Chapter of Mats.

Among those who attended was St. Dominic, with seven of his friars, who were on the way from Bologna to Rome. They stopped by to see what it was all about.

Another one of those who came was Cardinal Hugoline of Ostia. Francis had predicted that one day he would become Pope. And, so it was, he later became Gregory IX.

Those present were quiet and meek, praying and doing deeds of charity. The Groups made tents covered with mats all around, on the top and sides, and with rushes, and so it was called the Chapter of Mats. They slept on the ground or on straw.

Noblemen came and ordinary people, too; cardinals and bishops came to see the very holy and large gathering of saintly men; but, especially, they came to see Francis.

Francis greeted them and explained the word of God in a loud voice "As clear as a bugle," preaching whatever the Holy Spirit inspired him to say. He encouraged them to have reverence and obedience to Holy Mother Church; to have brotherly love; to pray for all the people of God; to have patience in adversity and temperance in prosperity; to be figures of chastity and to be at peace with God and all men; to love poverty and express humility and meekness, and have contempt for worldly things.

Under obedience he commanded them to have no care concerning anything to eat or drink, but to concentrate on praying and praising God and leave worldly worries to Christ who would take care of them.

St. Dominic felt consternation at this and thought his words imprudent. But soon people from Perugia, Spoleto, Foligno, Spello, Assisi and others from the surrounding countryside came with donkeys, mules and wagons loaded with bread and wine, beans and cheese and all good things to eat.

They also had among them those who were concerned for their brothers and sisters; they too brought things like pitchers, dishes, glasses and tablecloths and all such helpful items.

Knights and nobles went humbly about serving, so reverently it seemed as though they were serving, not the poor friars, but the apostles of our Lord Jesus Christ. When Dominic saw all this, he was overcome with remorse and begged Francis to forgive him.

When it was over, Francis sent them all back to their provinces comforted and filled with spiritual joy, with God's blessing and his own. To this day Franciscans hold this Chapter of Mats.

"To the glory of Our Lord Jesus Christ. May He be blessed! Amen."

*"A thought for us to take home might be to strip
ourselves of the inner garment of pride and
to put on the inner garment of Christ."*

He Discarded His Second Garment

I was thinking about poverty and wondering what to say. My mind began to tighten up and the more I tried to think about poverty the tighter it became. I leafed through the pages of the "Omnibus of Sources" of St. Francis and prayed to the Holy Spirit — nothing. Finally, in desperation, I banged the Omnibus shut and said, "All right, St. Francis, you're simply going to have to help me. I'm going to open this book and you will have to show me what you want me to say about poverty." This book has close to 2,000 pages.

I opened it and the first words my eyes lit on were, "He discarded his second garment." I was startled. That tied right in with poverty. I glanced up to the beginning of the passage and this is what I read:

"Until the work of restoring the church of Saint Damian was completed, blessed Francis still wore the garment of a hermit with a strap to serve as a belt, and he carried a staff and had sandals on his feet. Then, one day during the celebration of Mass he heard the words in which Christ bade his disciples to go out and preach, carrying neither gold nor silver, nor haversack for the journey, without staff, bread, or shoes, and having no second garment. After listening to the priest's explanation of these words of the Gospel, Francis, full of unspeakable joy, he exclaimed: 'this is what my whole heart desires to accomplish.'"

"He learned these words by heart, meditating on what he had heard and joyfully he started to put them into practice. He discarded his second garment, and from that day onwards he used no staff, shoes, or haversack; he kept one miserable tunic, and instead of the strap took a length of cord as a belt." (From: St. Francis' writings and Early Biographies, English Omnibus of Sources for the Life of St. Francis, Prologue to the Legend of our Blessed Father Francis, Chapter VIII #25)

To open this huge book on one of the passages of the Gospels that Francis himself had opened to was not only amazing, but it left me a bit shaken.

"He discarded his second garment," and "This is what my whole heart desires," is how he seemed to answer my demand, when I said, "Francis, you have to tell me what to say."

We know that as Franciscans we must, if we are sincere in our calling, practice the spirit of poverty. What does this mean? Everyone who talks about it says in effect, it doesn't mean we have to give up our worldly possessions. It means we have to strip ourselves of worldliness, sin, avarice, and anything that comes between us and Christ. That's very good, but wait a minute, aren't we holding back something from Christ? What are we holding back? Let's look at that again — "He discarded his second garment." I thought about it a long time.

When I was a candidate we had as spiritual assistant, the scholarly and very St. Francis-like Franciscan priest, Father Stephen Hardtegan, O.F.M. He told us not once but several times, "Poverty is to share." Here is one example: Give away the garments that are hanging in your closet, things that you are not using now but are keeping with the vague notion that you might want them some time. "Give them to the poor," he said. "Now!" It doesn't make any difference if they are practically new, expensive, or you have a soft spot in your heart for them — give them away.

That applies to all the other things in our life that are dear to us as well. Let us seriously think about those other things. It is for us to decide what we should do, whether it is to take that extra helping or give it to someone else or the desire to do what I want or to attend to the needs of someone else.

In our Rule, it says, in regard to charity, if we have a surplus above our own needs, there is not merely the choice but the duty of sharing . The rule of moderation and charity to which a Secular Franciscan pledges himself inclines him to take less than he may take; and in giving, to give more than he need give. This attitude opens up the way to various degrees of moderation and charity, all of which are a matter of choice and not of commandment. This is not the way of the world, it is true, but it is a Franciscan way of fostering the spirit of poverty.

This brings us back to the statement made in the beginning that most people say that it is the spirit of poverty that counts. And we agree that this is true, but the spirit of poverty is not just a spiritual thing; the spirit of poverty is fostered and begins by "doing something."

In a Christian's striving for perfection, you can't separate the physical aspect of it from the spiritual any more than you can separate the love of God from the love of our neighbor.

St. James said: *"Suppose there are brothers or sisters who need clothes and don't have enough to eat. What good is there in your saying to them, 'God bless you! Keep warm and eat well!' — If you don't give them the necessities of life?" (James 2: 15-16)*

So, what is St. Francis telling us when we point to the words, "He discarded his second garment?" Let's turn to our Rule again which states: "...Let them share these things (temporal goods) with their neighbors, bearing in mind that all temporal things — private property included — have been given to them by God not only for their own advantage but also that they may be administered well for the good of society. Moreover, let them in good time, will their property, with due regard for justice and charity."

This reminds us that nothing we have is really our own. In the manner of worldly thinking, things that we have are considered *ours*; *our* property is in *our* name and we buy and pay for things with *our* money. Can we call it *ours* — will we be able to take it with us when we die? If it were truly *ours* we would be able to take it with us. Remember, everything we have belongs to God and He kindly lends it to us for our needs while we live on this earth. Since it is His, we have an obligation to take good care of it and not abuse it; to share it with others, generously, as He is sharing it with us and finally, like the words of Christ in the Gospel, show Him on the day of judgment that we discarded our second garment.

"The Carceri —
"Experience of the Caves."

The Carceri

I was glancing through some of my back copies of the *Franciscan Herald* when these words on a front cover caught my eye: "The Carceri — Experience of the Caves." Before my May pilgrimage to Assisi, those words would not have caught my eye. But, since that pilgrimage ...!

The Carceri (meaning prisons) is one of the most beautiful to the eye and inspiring to the soul sanctuaries we had the privilege of visiting. It is high up on Mount Subasio where Francis and some of his brothers voluntarily imprisoned themselves in caves on the mountainside. They spent long hours in deep contemplation with God.

There is a mystery in the life of every Franciscan — a living in mystical fullness in the caves and in the Franciscan community. The caves and the community form a perfect sphere and the center is Christ.

The caves are our secret, silent place where we are alone with God, heart to heart with Him, and word to His Word. His Word to us in this secret place of ours is what tells us what to do, how to act, how to relate and how to serve in the community. It is from the caves in our own hearts that God directs us in our life in the world.

We are Franciscans because we have been chosen to follow and serve the Lord Jesus Christ and rebuild the Holy Roman Catholic Church in the spirit of our Holy Founder, St. Francis.

The center of our life in the world is Jesus who was born in the cave of our being in Holy Baptism, just as he was born in the cave in Bethlehem; and of Mary, His holy mother and in the Holy Spirit with the love of the Father. Astonishingly and marvelously, the "Babe of Bethlehem" is reborn in the caves of our human bodies, mingling His Flesh with our flesh and His Blood with our blood — our holy manna from heaven; He imbues our inmost being with His Divinity every time we receive Him in the Sacred Eucharist.

This is our consolation, our security, and our joy — this mystery of Jesus Christ, stooping to enter the caves of our heart. Our hearts would be empty and intolerable were it not for His dwelling within us.

This dwelling within us is with us all the time, it is our motivation to anything that is good. It is our bulwark of strength in times when we find it necessary to conquer both our weaker selves, and the unconquerable tribulations and heartaches of life.

It is our hope that our Franciscan Family will be a growing sign in the Church and in the world and that the eternal love God bears for us, who follow His humble servant, St. Francis, will enter into the caves of our heart and our community."

I cannot conceive a life in this world without being a Franciscan. It is the Lord's great gift and answer to our day. To which I add a fervent, Amen!

The Blessing of Brother Leo

The Tau Cross

"And the Lord said to him: Go through the midst of the city, through the midst of Jerusalem: and mark Thau upon the foreheads of the men that sigh and mourn for all the abominations that are committed in the midst." (Ezechiel 9: 4).

Thau is the last letter in the Hebrew alphabet and signifies a sign, or mark. St. Jerome and other interpreters think that the ancient Hebrew character had the form of a cross.

We see the Tau as a symbol of penance, of mercy and of preservation, as it had been a sign of mercy for Cain.

Pope Innocent said, "the Tau has exactly the same form as the cross to which Christ was nailed. It is only through the sign of the cross and the mortification of the flesh that people will obtain mercy and accept the life of the Crucified."

Pope Innocent had invoked the 4th Lateran Council, and had called upon all Christians to accept the Tau as a sign of the urgent need for spiritual renewal in the Church. He proclaimed the Tau to be a sign of humility because it is the last letter of the Hebrew alphabet.

St. Francis eagerly accepted this and at once made the Tau the symbol of his Orders. He traced it on himself before beginning each of his actions. He preferred it above all other symbols. He used it as his signature for his letters and writings. To Brother Leo he wrote: "May the lord bless you and keep you. May the Lord show His face to you and be merciful to you. May the lord lift up His countenance upon you and give you peace." And he added, "God bless you, Brother Leo!" and he sketched an image and drew a Tau over it as his signature. *(See page 87)*

Brother Leo wrote under Francis' signature, "This blessing was given to me, Brother Leo, by the blessed Francis, who wrote it in his own hand, and it is also his hand that drew the image and the Tau." This original letter of St. Francis to Brother Leo is one of three handwritings still in existence.

Francis painted the Tau on the walls of his brothers cells. On our pilgrimage to Assisi we saw one that he had painted in the small chapel of St. Mary Magdalene, at Fonto Colombo, where we had Mass on Ascension Thursday. This little chapel was built in the 12th Century. The Tau was up front, on the left wall near a window and was discovered in the early 1920's when the window was unblocked and opened to view after having been hidden for centuries.

A miracle is told by Thomas of Celano about a man who, after the death of St. Francis, had lost the use of his leg due to an abscess that would not heal. Francis appeared to him, touched the abscess with a small staff in the form of a Tau. The abscess burst and the man was healed.

San Damiano Crucifix

This crucifix you see above is very important to us, as Franciscans, because it had such a profound influence on St. Francis during his conversion process.

As Christ came to life and opened His lips and spoke to Francis at San Damiano, so should we let Him come alive in us, and speak to us.

Christ's mouth is small, and to me, it shows great tenderness and compassion. His great eyes seem almost to be pleading and seem to be drawing us to Him.

Jesus does not appear to be nailed to the cross, but rather to be standing out from it.

If we could, for the moment, remove His arms from where they are placed, we would see behind them the empty tomb.

You'll see, underneath His hands on either side, two angels; you can see that they are talking animatedly before the empty tomb. They are gesturing with their hands towards Jesus. These represent the angels who spoke to the holy women on the morning of the Resurrection.

Some figures are drawn small, some larger; this indicates their importance in this tableau. The small soldier with the lance on the left is the one who pierced Christ's side. On the right, a small figure in blue is a mocking Jew.

Painted much larger are: on the left, Mary, the Mother of Jesus, and the Apostle John. On the right is Mary Magdalene; Mary the mother of James, and the Roman Centurion. Note the centurion's two fingers raised as he proclaims, *"Truly this is Christ, the Son of God."* This was the first great acknowledgment by a Gentile that Jesus is the Son of God.

Above the shoulder of the Centurion is a small face, which is believed to be that of the artist himself, who sought a bit of immortality by sneaking his face into the picture.

Below, and obscure, is a painting of a rooster, if you look hard you can see his legs. I used a magnifying glass on the figure. This cock represents the one that crowed when Peter denied Christ, and it tells us, "Don't be too sure of yourself." Even Peter, who swore he would never leave Christ, denied Him three times before the cock crowed.

At the bottom, very obscure because of the antiquity of it, are some of the Apostles with upturned faces gazing at the ascending Lord. Remember the Gospel passage, *"You men of Galilee, why do you stand there idle? This Jesus, whom you have seen ascending, will come again."*

So, now look away up above Jesus' head to the red circle where Jesus is, indeed, ascending to heaven. In His hand He carries a slender cross, holding it as a scepter of triumph. Surrounding him is a choir of angels, singing His praises. (Fr. Kenan Morris, O.F.M., however said, this group are saints in heaven. He cited the two figures on either end of the cross shaft as figures of angels.) Father said there are 33 figures in the tableau. He said there might have been jewels at one time studded about the halo over Jesus' head.

On the Cross of Christ, above the halo, was placed the titulus, in which was written: JESUS OF NAZARETH, THE KING OF THE JEWS.

Above the circle with the ascending Jesus, in a half circle, is the right hand of the Father — see His two fingers outstretched.

At one of the churches, when I was in Italy we saw another crucifix that looked at first glance just like this one, but a second look showed it was not, because that one was of the dead Christ, his head sagging against His breast.

This one, the San Damiano Crucifix, is a cross of triumph; of victory over death and sin; over that empty tomb. It is the triumph of the risen Christ —

Christ ascending into Heaven, into the Presence of His Father.

The entire redemptive process of Jesus is in this Crucifix of San Damiano.

"Go and repair my church," He said to Francis. He is saying the same thing to us right now.

Notes

III The Franciscan Way of Life

Formation is our Foundation

(from an article written for the Southern Area Congress at Rollins College, June 1985)

Franciscan formation is a process wherein an ordinary Christian becomes an extraordinary disciple of Christ by following the Gospel the way St. Francis of Assisi did.

I'm sure all of you have heard many times that one of the most important things in the life of a Secular Franciscan is Ongoing Formation — the down-to-earth, nitty-gritty, taking-the-bull-by-the-horns process of ACTIVATING in our lives what we have been reading, hearing, and praying about.

You can go through a Franciscan textbook as an inquirer and candidate; you can read every book you can get your hands on about St. Francis; you can read the Bible every day of your life; but, none of these adds much of anything to your formation growth unless you put the message into practice in your daily living.

Pope Pius XII, in a talk to the Secular Franciscans of Italy in 1956, said, "You must not just KNOW about the life of St. Francis; but, you must FORM yourselves in the spirit of his message." Father Benet Fonck, O.F.M., said "Without formation, Franciscans don't happen."

Formation has been likened to a school of perfection, a school where one aspires to "be perfect as our heavenly Father is perfect."

In this school of perfection, the candidate is not just LEARNING this new way of life; he or she is undergoing an APPLIED learning experience, an on-the-job training procedure

Once candidates are committed to this new way of life, they are never again the same. Candidates, no longer their own boss, can be compared to recruits entering an army.

In this army of St. Francis no one is drafted, each person enters as a volunteer. We don't make our own rules. We operate under the tried and true "Rule" set forth well over 750 years ago by St. Francis himself. And he, as we all know so well, got it straight from the gospels.

What do we mean by that?

We mean this: Die to self; to our own egos; to our desire to have everyone go along with our way of thinking or doing what we want all the time.

The basis of our formation is just that, a dying to self and *metanoia*, a radical inner conversion.

In this army of the gospel way of life, we can get a lot farther as individuals if we motivate ourselves to a deep-seated sense of patriotism towards the great Franciscan family. It means getting a feeling of loyalty to the Church — a gung-ho attitude about God and St. Francis!

New candidates actually must form themselves; but, they do not do it alone, they have instructors who urge them on and members of the fraternity who guide them by their example and friendly acceptance.

Formation is Ongoing

We all need to read, read, read. Thus we will grow in the knowledge of the Franciscan way of life. But, growing in knowledge is NOT formation.

Formation is USING what you are learning; using it out there in the world where you knock elbows with a great assortment of temperaments — that's formation. That is your on-the-job training and until you do that you will not grow much in the Franciscan way of life.

This applies not only to the candidates; but, to all the professed members as well.

I have been in the happy situation in my fraternity of having a few professed members attend my instruction sessions for the new people, including, thanks be to God, council members. This example of dedication and caring from our leaders and professed members is a tremendous boost, not only for the candidates, but for all of us.

A good Franciscan example, by all members of the fraternity, is the best teacher of all. It is worth a thousand instructions, a thousand books. It leads and it says, "This is the way, come follow me."

I remember at a large gathering of Secular Franciscans in St. Augustine several years ago, the late Ralph Fenton, S.F.O., our then provincial president, in a talk to fraternity ministers and directors of formation, said, "we should not come at the candidates like a drill sergeant." And finally, let me repeat the theme of what I have said before: We should lead, invite and show them by our example, with our actions saying: "see, I'm not asking you to do something I'm not doing myself."

Formation Director

Formation Director can be scary for both the candidate and a newly appointed director of formation. In many cases directors of formation didn't ask for the job.

One fatal day, one finds oneself looking down in disbelief at one's lap where the role of director of formation has just been dropped, Kerplunk! It's a bit shattering to say the least, but after a period of stunned immobility, there is the gathering of oneself together and running, not walking, for the nearest help.

Where is this help?

Where does any child run for help but to an understanding father and a loving mother — to God and to Mary. That is the first and the biggest step forward we need to take. It is a long, unwavering step into our prayer life.

We need to take a journey inward, away down into our mysterious inner self and get acquainted with ourselves. Down there we can, as Francis did, fall head-over-heels in love with Jesus Christ. This is what we are all about as followers of St. Francis — people crazy in love with Jesus.

I'll never forget the first time I came across the passage by Thomas of Celano. (I've said this before, but it needs repeating). He was saying, *"Francis was a man so deeply in love with Christ that he had Jesus in his eyes, Jesus in his ears, Jesus in his mouth, Jesus in his hands, Jesus in every cell of his body, Jesus, Jesus, Jesus!"* Before I finished reading that, I was goose bumps all over.

To have this feeling is to have one of the greatest gifts God can bestow. It is the center, out of which EVERYTHING in our lives should radiate.

We must truly believe what Jesus said, "Without me you can do nothing."

Ah, but with Jesus we can do so much. We can plunge into the awesome responsibility of being a director of formation.

Directors of formation, and those who instruct candidates are a terrific and privileged breed.

If you are chosen to be one, rejoice and be glad, even as you moan inwardly that you can't do it.

Thank God, who saw fit to call you to this important work in the Franciscan family; because, the Franciscan who benefits the most is yourself, in your own personal formation.

To be a good, dedicated director or instructor is a gift of God. God is at your beck and call, and brings Jesus to your side to guide you in this great opportunity to delve heart and soul into the mysteries of what made Francis so great — this Francis who was so great that his name is renowned among Catholics, Protestants, non-believers and even atheists throughout the world.

If you are sincere and dedicated in this work (and this goes for those of you who are in any kind of Franciscan work) you cannot stand still. You cannot, because the preparation of the work itself will bring you to a closeness to God you never knew before.

It can grow to be so deep-seated that at times you have an overpowering desire to hug yourself because of the great wonder of what is going on inside you.

The mechanics of formation are important. They should be flexible enough at each session, whether it be candidate instruction or ongoing formation, to fit the needs of that particular day and group. They must not be allowed to become monotonous. They need to be dressed up in a new outfit every now and then — a springtime look — a new Easter bonnet.

"The Holy Father says,
'Holy Poverty flees from luxury.'"

Franciscan Poverty

How can we define Franciscan Poverty? We can, by picturing a stark, desolate moment in History. Close your eyes a minute and think of the summit of Calvary. See the poor Man Christ standing there literally stripped to the skin, the cross flat on the ground beside Him waiting for His almost nude body to be nailed to it.

Next, think of St. Francis, "the little poor man." To him Poverty was a strip act, too — a stripping off anything and everything that is worldly and not Christ-like.

Now, let us think of ourselves, we who are striving for Franciscan perfection. For us, too, poverty can be and must be a strip act, a simple, steady endeavor to completely strip ourselves down to be Christ-like.

To some degree, poverty must be practiced by every Christian. It is a self-cultivated virtue that frees us from a reaching out for and grasping after things of the world. If we practice poverty we will be left wide open to the inflowing way of Christ.

What about money in our lives? Money is not evil in itself. The old saying, "Money is the root of all evil," is a variation of the true quotation used once by St. Peter after Christ's ascension into Heaven, *"the love of money is the root of all evil."* Money can buy good things and it can buy bad things; it can uplift and it can corrupt; it can buy things we need or things that are frivolous. It can buy a bowl of rice for a starving child or it can buy a useless trinket for a child.

Real poverty comes from the heart. That is where it takes seed and as it sprouts and begins to grow, it manifests itself in outward signs and deeds.

The love of money is the root of Evil — with a capital E. It is rampant in the world and when it is coupled with a lust for power it becomes lethal. It becomes GREED, SELF-LOVE and SELF-GRATIFICATION. It becomes, a THING TO ADORE, an IDOL.

Money, on the other hand, when not used as a god, but as a gift of God, takes its proper place in life. It becomes something necessary and even pleasantly and mildly desirable in our lives. It needs only to be disciplined by the virtue of poverty. Poverty frees us from inordinate human desires and makes room within us for God's love to enter in and help us put on the brakes, when we don't discipline ourselves.

How, in a practical way can we cultivate the spirit of Poverty? Let's take a good hard look at the things we buy? How much of what we buy is sheer waste buying? Look in any store you go into, many counters display goods that are needed and useful; but, look at the counter upon counter of the absolute junk with a high price tag on it.

How about the senseless waste of useful things only half used, things quickly tired of and discarded; things abused, carelessly broken, or allowed to rust and go bad unused? How about food — garbage cans that are partially filled with wasted, edible food?

How about keeping up with the Joneses: How many plunges in over our foolish heads have been made with this one? Living beyond one's means is living a lie. How about our priorities? Do we have the right to buy a Cadillac, for instance, while all we can afford to do is feed the kids beans, spaghetti, or rice? Let's take a look at the other side of the coin; how about buying the kids everything and anything they want while denying the basic needs of some other member of the family or neighbors; these actions give the kids the idea that the world owes them a living and it doesn't make any difference whether anyone else has anything or not.

How about panic buying: Rumor has it there is going to be a shortage of beef, gasoline, or toilet paper; or that prices are going up on this or that. Buy! Stock up! Six months later the trash cans begin to collect the unneeded, unwanted, unusable, deteriorated excess; while somewhere, someone did go without because the panic buying did create a shortage.

How about the energy crunch: Are we doing our bit to save energy? How about electricity? Are we still wasting it right and left? Do we go about splashing lights all over the place, turning on six lights where one would do or leaving them turned on in every room in the house when we are using only one room, or failing to turn them off when we no longer need them?

These are a few examples and the examples are a dime a dozen. We can look at our own situation and, ask ourselves questions and size up our own spirit of poverty. Just how far afield are we from the spirit of poverty in our daily buying and living habits?

At this point, strangely enough, the subject of the fraternity *common fund* is brought up and we realize that everyone should give something regularly, even if he or she doesn't attend a meeting. No set amount is ever assessed and it need not be a great deal. Each person gives what he feels is a right amount for him or her to give. It doesn't make any difference what anyone else gives — everyone is responsible for himself or herself.

The donations are secret. They are not recorded to divulge ones habits; the total amount is recorded at each monthly meeting. The common fund is used for Fraternity expenses — supplies; an occasional guest speaker; sometimes travel expenses to a convention; charity to needy members; regional fund, and apostolic projects. The contribution should not be taken from ordinary personal spending needs and habits. It should be a personal part of our own spirit of poverty and our affection for and concern for our fraternity and its members, and it should be given in a spirit of sacrifice and love for the Franciscan Order and for the Church, and so, for Christ Himself. Thus, it becomes Christ-centered.

So much for the common fund which, as you see, is related to our spirit of poverty.

Another concrete element of poverty is the most common one of all, the tragic polarization of the haves and the have-nots, the all too common, worldwide poverty of human deprivation.

Consider the situation here in America, where, on the one hand we see so many of our tables laden with a super-abundance of good nourishing food, while on the other hand we see a tragic picture (perhaps it is just a picture in a mission magazine, which we know is the real McCoy) of great big eyes in a bony face of a child out there somewhere who is undernourished or even starving. And, here we have a closet crammed full of clothing, warm and cool clothing, some are sensible things and others are not so sensible; while out there somewhere there is a person so thinly clad he is shivering in the cold. How do we reconcile these contrasts with Christ's own words, *"Come ... for I was hungry and you gave me to eat ... naked and you clothed me ..."* Or, the converse of that — Christ's warning words, *"Depart from me ... for I was hungry and you gave me nothing to eat ... Naked and you did not cloth me..."*

These are some of the really hard things we each should ponder sincerely and work out in our own way, in our own consciences, in order to reconcile what we have, with what we give to those who do not have.

Now, we come to the deeply spiritual poverty that is the Poverty of Christ.

St. Francis, said, "Poverty is a royal virtue, it is shone so brightly in the King and queen," — Christ and Our Lady. He said, "Understand that Poverty is a choice way of salvation; the fruit it bears is manifold, and rare are they who know it well." He said, "If Christ lived it, I must live it." And, if Francis lived it, we must live it if our goal is Franciscan perfection; by doing so we can continue the poverty of Christ on earth today. For us, who are followers of St. Francis the poor man, Christ must never stop walking through the world.

Jesus chose to be born poor, why?

The Spirit of poverty is a mental condition, or should we say conditioning? It is another of our spiritual freedoms — freedom from greed, especially greed for money and power and position beyond our proper status. It is contentment with, and gratefulness to God for what we have; for *"giving us this day our daily bread."* The Holy Father says, "Holy Poverty flees from luxury."

What is this luxury? It is an unrestrained indulgence in costly living. It is the gratification of desire for the empty pomp of living. Poverty flees this emptiness and seeks the fullness that is in Christ. Poverty loves little things, and is happy with the ordinary things of life. It enjoys having a good home, a few beautiful things, music, flowers, time-saving appliances, all on the level of our means to pay for them. These are looked upon as joyous things lent to us by God for a happy existence, and never for the purpose of showing off, or, of going someone else a bit better. Our Franciscan rule states, "In all things let the members avoid extremes of cost and style, observing the golden mean suited to each one's station in life." Franciscan poverty, instead of enslaving us to things, makes things our slaves. We choose things and use them wisely; we do not let things use us. Our attitude should be, I can take them or leave them. Poverty is full trust in the Providence of God.

More on Franciscan Poverty

We have Franciscan guidelines and we have Francis' message — two key points, love God, and Gospel poverty — these permeated Francis' entire life.

We have poverty — simple living, humility, frugality, sharing and serving. Jesus said, *"If you would be perfect, go sell what you have and give to the poor. Then come follow me."* Another time, He and some of the disciples were watching people place donations into the temple treasury. Some of the rich were giving lavishly. But along comes this scene:

The woman was elderly, and weary;
Her brown eyes were blurry and teary.

Her figure was bent and forlorn;
Her dress was faded and torn.

Her skin was the color of straw;
Her hand reached out like a claw.

The fingers clutched something tight,
Then, into the treasury dropped the widow's mite.

These pictures flashed through my head,
It was all that she had, Jesus said.

What message do these pictures convey to us?

Do we go rushing out, as Francis and his followers did, and sell all we have and give it to the poor? We do not. We use our common sense.

If you have nothing, you can share nothing. You cannot even take care of yourselves and those dependent on you. You become a burden if you make yourself poor.

The answer is: We need to be good stewards of what God has given us — using, sharing and serving others with care.

"St. Francis said, 'All brothers ought to preach by their actions.'"

Preaching by good example

To become a true "Secular Franciscan" one has to assume, if one has not already done so, Christian adulthood. We are to not act like a child and do something because we are told to do it, but to do something because we see something needs to be done.

We stepped into this "adult" world, to a certain extent, when we received the sacrament of Confirmation. When we received this sacrament we voluntarily became active in the Body of Christ — His Church and our Church.

Christ said, *"Go into the whole world and preach the Gospel to everyone."* He did not mean just the twelve Apostles. He meant all of us, down through the ages. We are apostles, doing missionary work right in our own home, in our own back yard, in our own neighborhood and wherever we go.

The apostolate of Secular Franciscans is, as a rule, in the secular world where we live. It is in this area that we are able to move about effectively, either individually or as a member of a group or organization, helping our brothers and sisters in their and our pilgrimage through life. How much or how little of this sort of apostolate an individual does depends on his circumstance, his ability, and his dedication. Some simply are not able to do much and others can do very much; but, everyone is able to be a witness to Christ, whether he is confined to a bed or a world traveler. It has been said, somewhere, "No man is an island." Every man comes into some contact, briefly or otherwise, with other people, and each single contact is an opportunity to show Christ to others.

One of St. Francis' mottoes was, not to live for himself alone, but to help others. Even an invalid in bed can do this; he can say, "Good morning." He can smile and cooperate, and say, "Thank you." He can pray.

Words attributed to St. Francis were, "All brothers ought to preach by their actions." The most basic apostolate for any Christian is the apostolate of good example. How can anyone hope to draw others to Christianity if he does not act Christ-like in his daily living? We should act always in the belief that what we are doing and saying is having an effect on those with whom we come in contact. Most of the time we won't know whether we are having an effect or not. Maybe the effect isn't taking place at all. We may never know the answer to that. We don't need to worry about it if we establish a pattern of good example.

If we are going to be hooked on a habit, let it be a good habit. If we look back on our own lives we can think of many good habits, sometimes seemingly insignificant, that someone like our parents, teacher, friend, priest, or nun had. They may not have realized themselves that they had it, nor did we know at the time; but; it crept into our minds and stuck. It is the seemingly insignificant, routine, good habits; persistently done over and over that have a lasting effect on someone. They stick to his subconscious mind many years before becoming activated some time in the future.

"Bear"
and
"Forebear."

Franciscans are People of Peace

The Secular Franciscan Rule and Constitutions admonish Secular Franciscans to, "make the greatest endeavor to restore and promote the spirit of charity and peace." Jesus said *"Blessed are the peacemakers."* Followers of St. Francis and those since his time have greeted one another with the phrase "Pax et Bonum!" — "Peace and Goodness to you!" St. Francis used this greeting.

So, one of the Franciscan apostolates is peace and peace-making. Peace in this sense does not mean the absence of problems, temptations or suffering. What it does mean is the inner serenity that comes from Christ-centered living, which is generated within us, extends out in our relationship with others.

In order to be a peacemaker one has to be humble and charitable. He must aim at truth in any given situation. This is all-important. Truth! We must be honest with ourselves in our inmost thoughts. We must try not to be alibi artists, making excuses for our weaknesses, lapses and mistakes — not to ourselves or to anyone else.

We must face the truth if we are to be apostles of peace and good will. Someone once said, "The man who excuses himself accuses himself." What we really are will surface sooner or later. Sooner or later a phony will be recognized.

In the interests of peace we must be patient and forbearing. We could, with profit, make inseparable companions of two well known bears, "Bear" and "Forebear."

We should also try to learn the art of silence — there is a time when it is better to be silent than to speak.

God's peace can sometimes come only through a galling, deliberate and flattening of one's own ego. To insist on one's own point of view is disruptive to peace and really quite unimportant. Sometimes when we know we are right it is better not to insist on proving it. We can have within ourselves the peace of knowing we are right; that Jesus knows it and that in silence we are keeping His peace; and really, what difference does it make anyway — sometimes, even in war, peace is brought about by surrender. To give in with dignity in order to keep peace, as long as no Christian principle is in jeopardy, is the Christ-like way.

Prayer of a Bonded Servant

May I be your disciple, Jesus,
Work for you and not ask for pay?
Just a volunteer slave to you, Master,
From morning to night, day by day.

Not counting the cost, nor the labor,
Just happy to serve as I do;
Not giving a thought to vacations;
How could I wish a vacation from you.

Just a slave in your household forever,
Giving my heart all out to you there.
Not wanting another thing, Jesus,
But to know I'm secure in your care.

"From Gospel to Life and from Life to Gospel?"

Discipleship

"Discipleship. That's a costly word," Deacon Henry Libersat said.

"A bonded servant," he said, "A voluntary slave."

"A disciple never takes a vacation from his master. When he comes in from a day's work in the field, he gets right at getting his master's dinner, rather than sitting down to rest or get his own meal first."

Those are thoughts that are hard to take. They are alien to our natural human Instincts.

Am I bonded to you, Jesus?

Do I wait on you before myself?

Am I your disciple? If I haven't been up to now, I want to start to be now.

I don't want a vacation from you. I want to serve you out in the marketplace and when I come into your presence.

Isn't that exactly our status as Secular Franciscans?

We live in the world, but we are also members of your household.

We are your servants.

We go from serving you personally (prayer) to doing your work in the marketplace and then back we come into your household again to serve you personally once more, again in our prayers, in which we give you our undivided attention. This is in our Rule, "From Gospel to Life and from Life to Gospel?"

"The 'Franciscan Way of Life'
is to begin to feel the
great joy and the marvel
of how it can bring you
into a closer intimacy and
greater love of Jesus Christ."

Franciscan Apostolates

Dear Brothers and Sisters I would like you to become really aware of yourselves and understand what Franciscanism is all about and not just depend on the words of other people. I want you to begin or if you have already begun, to intensify your own feeling about what this "Franciscan Way of Life" is and to begin to feel the great joy and the marvel of how it can bring you into a closer intimacy and greater love of Jesus Christ. I want you to begin right now to stand on your own two feet and be dedicated to this mission.

1. The Duty of the Apostolate
"God has not called you for your own sake alone; but, also to save others."

(a) A responsible adult does things not because he is asked to do them, but because they need to be done.

(b) As baptized children in the Church, we work for our own personal salvation. Later we receive the Sacrament of Confirmation and grow up and feel responsible for the great family of people of which we are a part.

(c) We are to *"go and preach to all nations."* We are to share our faith with others.

How? For most of us, it is by example. St. Francis said, "All brothers and sisters should preach by their actions."

2. The Apostolate is Good Example.
(a) We may think we have little influence on others. Don't believe it! Even as we have been influenced by the good of others, like mothers, fathers and teachers; so too, we may, unknown to ourselves, influence others to be good. Someone once said, "What you are thunders so loud I can't hear what

you say."

(b) We should always call on Christ to influence what we do and how we should react in any given situation.

3. The Apostolate of Peace.

(a) Blessed are the peacemakers. Pax et Bonum! Peace and Goodness to you.

(b) Peace. What is it? Peace is in the heart, despite physical or mental suffering or tragedy. It is found in Christ on the Cross. Christ is peace. Without Christ there is turmoil! Peace is seeing eye to eye with Christ.

(c) Peace is not the absence of trouble, problems, suffering or temptation. Peace is Christ in our hearts, in our thoughts and in our wills. It is our responsibility to conform our will to the Omniscient One.

(d) Peacemakers should be humble, charitable, prudent and patient. One must be ready to be silent when words are futile.

(e) One must not be unbending. Peace may have to be made by surrender, not of a principle; but, by yielding to the preference of another.

4. The Apostolate of Personal Holiness.

(a) We want holiness for ourselves and for the whole world. Holiness is not a private affair. Holiness is social because it consists of charity to all men.

(b) Holiness is apostolic, not in devotion alone; but, in action and in involvement in projects.

5. The Apostolate as Franciscans.

(a) Francis' philosophy was, not to live for himself alone, but to live for the benefit of others.

(b) Christ said, *"I came, not to be served, but to serve."* We see again the Franciscan apostolate following closely the Gospel way which is Christ's way. His way is what He said, what He did and what He taught us while He lived on earth.

(c) Christ did not come for the private benefit of St. Francis or anyone else. He came to make all men his brothers, and for this task, the help of all Franciscans is welcomed and necessary.

(d) The Secular Franciscan Order must be actively apostolic. The primary purpose is personal holiness, but the secondary and equally essential purpose is the active apostolate. The Secular Franciscan Order is not merely a devotional society. Christ works through us, and He succeeds only to the degree that we work for Him.

6. The Apostolate To Those Within The Church.

(a) We are the Church and we are either the glory or the shame of it.

(b) We can spoil what God has made, so there must be a purifying within ourselves.

(c) Secular Franciscans should, in their daily life, strive to lead others by good example, including piety and good works. It should be with kindness — kindness to converts, to fellow parishioners, to those who have strayed, to those who are confused and to those who are strangers in our parish.

7. The Apostolate to the Church and Christianity

(a) Keep humble in all things. We should know that all the good works we do are the result of God working through us. As St. Paul said, *"if we are to boast, let us boast in Jesus Christ in whatever we do."*

(b) Secular Franciscans should be informed Catholics. Do not be timid in answering questions about your Faith. If we feel we do not know enough to answer questions, we have an obligation to learn more about our faith, both for our own sake and for the sake of others. We should: Read Diocesan newspapers, religious books and magazines; attend religious discussions and be ecumenical.

8. The Apostolate of Defending the Church.

(a) We must defend the Church against the Devil. We should know who he is and what tactics he uses, and know that only through the power of God can we conquer him. It is by fasting, prayer and charity that this can be done.

(b) We must defend the Church against the world — against the evil in the world. It is sometimes in the voice of a crowd; sometimes in the voice of one
person; sometimes openly and brazenly and sometimes slyly, hiding behind friendship, behind beauty, talent and popularity.

How? It is by standing up for what is right; by being not just against something, but for something. It is not condemning people but condemning evil acts and error. It is by encouraging and understanding others, by showing your love for them as children of God.

(c) We must defend the Church against ignorance, the seat of error.

(d) We must proclaim that what is true, is true! Do not be afraid of the truth.

9. The Apostolate of Social Justice.

St. Francis was a social reformer. In the earliest Rule no one was allowed to bear arms to be used against any person. Today the defense of one's country or self is allowed by law of the Church.

Secular Franciscans should:

(a) Pay all debts because it is just.

(b) Give or take a just price for goods and services.

(c) Promote peace between members of different social classes.

(d) Better the conditions of the poorer classes.

(e) Support and encourage the middle classes.

(f) Honor agricultural and manual workers.

(g) Strive to better the social and political world.

(h) Promote Interracial justice. We must see Christ in brothers and sisters of all races, even when we might be blamed for supporting them and suffer because of it.

(i) Have concern for all human rights. A Franciscan is his brother's keeper.

(j) Not be an isolated or selfish Christian.

(k) Work for the body and the soul of all mankind.

10. The Apostolate of the Laity in Society.

Secular Franciscans have responsibilities.

(a) To try to produce a moral society.

(b) To try to produce a society whose institutions are morally sound. These institutions are: Political, economic, educational, family, recreational, and religious. We should try to foster the Christian ideal in these six institutions.

(c) As parents, to Christianize their family life. The basis for a Social Apostolate starts in each individual in his or her own family where there is prayer and good example. This must come before all other apostolic work. After the family, if there is time, they can be involved in outside-the-family apostolates.

We must do what we can and look for opportunities, even though it is in a small way, to make the world a better place to live.

Remember, many a good movement dies because people loose heart. Franciscans should never lose heart.

Notes

"Our actions tell the true story, loud and clear."

Being Polite

To be a Franciscan is nothing more than being polite and considerate to God and to man. It is practicing what we preach. It is living the "Peace Prayer," not just saying the words. To be a good Franciscan one doesn't have to go about telling how much one loves Jesus. Our actions, performed quietly and in a neighborly way, will let other people know that Christ lives in our hearts.

St. Francis was a very polite little man — little in stature, that is.

How polite are we? How many of us listen to the other person? It is very impolite not to listen. It is impolite to be unnecessarily insistent. Too often our attitude is, "this is the way it is. I am right. You are wrong," and even as we recite the words, "Lord, make me an instrument of your peace," we are insisting on our own point of view.

How does it come out? Do we change the minds of our, shall we say, opponent, to our way of thinking? Rarely. The other fellow goes on thinking his way and we do the same, and amid the crackling and popping of words, peace is short circuited.

Franciscanism is Christ-in-action, through us. It isn't glibly saying the "Peace Prayer," it is doing what the prayer says. It is basically being polite and tactful. If someone says, "It happened Monday," we do not have to cut in with, "It wasn't Monday, it was a Tuesday." What difference does it make whether it was Monday or Tuesday. Sometimes by not arguing a point, where we think we are right, we save ourselves from having to eat crow later when we find out that we were wrong all the time.

Too often we are not exactly polite with Christ. There are a lot of things that Christ said that we don't listen to. Do we ask ourselves, "does what He is saying apply to me?" or do we say, "It applies exactly to so-and-so."

For example, there is the episode when Christ spoke about the Pharisee and the Publican in the Temple. The Pharisee in the temple was conspicuously in front "Lord-Lording" all over the place while the Publican meekly, with bowed head, stood away in the back. *"Lord, I thank thee I am not like that sinner there,"* cries the Pharisee rolling his eyes piously back towards the target of his disapproval. While the Publican quietly says, *"Lord, have mercy on me a sinner."*

In which category would Jesus put me, I wonder? Would He see me in the Pharisee or in the Publican? Maybe I'd better take time out and think about these things that Jesus is saying. Maybe I'd better be more polite and listen to him. Maybe I'd better put my feet in the shoes of the other guy and see if they fit my feet.

When Jesus said, *"Let your light shine before men,"* He, by no means meant we should, like the Pharisee, point our finger accusingly in the direction of someone else while patting ourselves on the back. What we say about ourselves, as the song says, "... ain't necessarily so." Our actions tell the true story, loud and clear.

"Lord make me an instrument of your peace."

"... the spirit of obedience
is remembering Christ
as He stooped to wash
the feet of the Apostles. "

Obedience

Secular Franciscans do not take vows of poverty, chastity or obedience, but we do definitely commit ourselves to the practice of these virtues.

The very essence of a Secular Franciscan vocation is obedience. There is no way we can follow the Gospel Way without being obedient to HIS way, HIS truth and HIS life.

In St. Matthew's Gospel we have the Sermon on the Mount. In this, and in other teachings of Christ, Jesus actually seems to throw out the old law; for instance, the curing of people on the Sabbath or the disciples not washing their hands before eating the grain in the field. This is not God's basic law.

There is the very detailed Mosaic Law in which God says, do this and don't do that. He spells it out in great detail. Why? Because He was dealing with an immature, illiterate, follow-the-leader class of spiritually undeveloped people. "Do this and it is a sin." "Don't do that and it is a sin." They were like "dumb driven cattle." When Jesus appeared on the scene, He was saying, we are going to do an about-face — we are going to become mature spiritual people; we are not going to destroy the old law, we are going to fulfill it.

The Ten Commandments are still a major factor in determining what a sin is and what it is not. Now, instead of ruling by fear, we are going to motivate by love. We are going to base the whole thing on two basic Commandments: First, love God (accept His love and give it back to Him). Second, extend this love of His that is now in us by giving it out to our brothers and sisters in the world where we live. You and everyone else should do this out of your own individual intellect, heart, free will and conscience, which God gave you.

He does not leave us orphans altogether in this responsibility. To help us He gives us His Church — His Vicar on earth, our beloved Roman Pontiff; His bishops; His pastors; His Secular Franciscan Order, etc., etc. And the only way these "gifts" and "aids" of His are going to help us is through our obedience. We listen to them and we follow them; not in a childish way, but in a mature, common sense way as maturing, eager-to-learn adults.

So, what is obedience for a Secular Franciscan? It is our conscience in action; it is loyalty to the Church, the Pope, our Bishop and our pastor; it is adhering to Canon Law; it is obeying the Commandments of God — all of them, including the Commandments of the Church. It is obeying the Rule and Constitutions of the Secular Franciscan Order which embraces attendance at the regular monthly meetings; holding office when it is required of us; contributing to the spiritual and material welfare of the fraternity; cooperating in apostolic projects and practicing Franciscan virtues — self-denial, self-control, self-discipline and selflessness.

For parents, particularly with young children, obedience also embraces remembering who is the adult and who is the child. In the family, this means teaching their children the basics of the Catholic religion at home, including their prayers, and commanding their obedience, etc.

Have you ever thought, now that you are an adult, what it means to be obedient — I mean, obedient in a broad sense? Is it nodding our heads this way and that way? Is it saying, "yes sir" or "no sir?" Is it following blindly? Is it stumble-bumbling along and thinking, "father so-and-so says this certain thing is a sin so I must not do it" or, "Father so-and-so says this isn't a sin, so I can do it?" Listen to what St. Francis says about blind obedience:

"If anyone of the ministers commands any brother to do anything against our way of life or against his conscience, the brother should not be held to obey him, for that is not obedience if a fault or sin is committed by it."

We have to remember, in all these instructions designed to point us in the direction of spiritual perfection, that we must not say to ourselves, "why, this particular thing applies exactly to her or to him." We must say instead, "does it apply to me, and if so, how?" We must say, "I am responsible for my actions, not for hers or his, except insofar as my bad example or good example may possibly affect her or him." Not one of us can say, "I'm not guilty, but she or he is."

Each one of us, to be serious about this and really honest with ourselves and with Christ. We must look hard, accusingly, and truthfully into own motives, emotions, and actions. Only then can we really start moving ourselves in the direction of spiritual perfection. Believe me it isn't easy! We are, I am afraid, only too willing to hold ourselves blameless while giving the other guy a big black mark. Such is contrary to the truth and we are only kidding and lying to ourselves. We do not gain spiritual perfection by lying to ourselves about ourselves.

Obedience, like humility, is a deliberate attempt on our part to rein in the ever present vice of pride.

We can think of obedience as being desirable for a number of reasons. First, and the best one of all is, Christ practiced it. St. Paul said, *"He became obedient unto death, even death on the cross."* "He came," He said, *"to do His Father's work."* *"Father,"* He cried out in the Garden of Gethsemani, *"if it be possible let this chalice pass from me. But not my will but yours be done."*

Again, another reason for obedience, is to curb the vice of pride which is a part of every human nature. Obedience helps to put us in a proper relationship with everyone, whether they be above us or below us. They are our brothers and sisters in Christ. Christ said, *"I came to serve, not to be served,"* so we should all do and say the same thing.

To be obedient we need not be subservient. We need only to be decently humble and cooperative and respectful of the rights and opinions of others and be willing to lend a hand where we can properly do so.

An obedient person is a responsible person. He is, to borrow an expression, "childlike" but not "childish." He is a spiritual child — a child of God.

We of the Secular Order of St. Francis must keep in mind, always, that before we were Franciscans we were Catholics and the better Franciscans we become the better Catholics we will grow to be. Following the way of St. Francis makes us better Catholics.

Franciscans, as are all Catholics, are subject to the authority of the Pope, the bishops and the priests of their parishes. The spirit of obedience should prompt us to have a spirit of wholehearted cooperation toward each member of the fraternity, and toward the Franciscan Community as a whole.

This includes willingly abiding by the rules and regulations insofar as they promote the good of all members; and lending, what we might call, an "obedient" ear to the suggestions and thoughts of others. Everyone's opinion and suggestion should be welcome at all times.

The spirit of obedience in a fraternity is a self-denial and a self-giving by each individual member for the good of all the other members in the fraternity.

It is a willingness to abide by the wishes and decisions of the majority, as befits any democratic organization.

Finally, the spirit of obedience is remembering Christ as He stooped to wash the feet of the Apostles. It is an opening of our ears and minds to take in His words, *"I have given you an example that as I have done, you do also."*

St. Francis founded his Orders on a rock — the rock of obedience to

Christ's Church. Why was St. Francis so insistent on obedience to the authority of the Church? First, by following the true teachings of the Church his followers would not run the risk of falling into heresy. Second, in addition to poverty and chastity he wanted to provide them with a third means of purification, a liberating self-denial and the subjection of their wills to the doctrines and dogmas of the Church.

Secular Franciscans do not take a vow of obedience as do the religious of the First, Second and Third Order Regulars; but, if they are to aim at spiritual perfection, they would do well to cultivate a desirable measure of the spirit of obedience.

Following the way of St. Francis is taking ourselves by the scruff of the neck and telling ourselves, "look here! You see what Christ did. You hear what He said. You have His example to go by, now let's do it."

*"One thing is absolute,
and that is, we must have
penance in our lives.
We simply cannot make it
through the 'Pearly Gates'
with out it."*

Penance

As Franciscans we are, or should be, constantly striving for spiritual perfection, the Gospel way. To this end, let us try to revitalize the part true Penance has in this struggle for spiritual perfection.

One thing is absolute, and that is, we must have penance in our lives. We simply cannot make it through the "Pearly Gates" without it. We have sinned and do things all the time that we should not do. And, there are sins of omission, things we should do that we do not do. We can't just write these sins off even though we are sorry for them. We *must* do penance. How? Let's poke around in this area a little while and consider just what penance can do for us.

One thing penance can do is act like a buffer between us and the tricky conniving of Satan. We call this buffer against sins that we might stumble into this afternoon, tomorrow, next month, or next year "Penance for the Future."

What is "Penance for the Future?" Simply, it is a way of helping us insure ourselves against future sin. To get this insurance or to acquire any insurance we have to pay a premium. The premium is self-denial and self-denial leads to self-discipline and self-control. Penance is made perfect only by the mastery of these virtues. Don't ever underestimate their worth. It takes a terrific amount of self-discipline to kiss a leper; to bear intense pain; to submit to a slap in the face by life and to say "no" to a temptation when we are simply dying to say "yes."

Jesus said, *"If anyone wishes to come after me let him deny himself, take up his cross and follow me."*

All right, think about those words a minute: *"deny himself."* Isn't that self-denial straight from Christ's own lips?

His words, *"Let him take up his cross and follow me,"* is discipline and self-control, as He taught. Isn't this what it means to live the Gospel way?

Now, the only way in the world we can cultivate these virtues is by persistent and arduous training. It is sometimes a grueling, day-in-and-day-out forcing ourselves to practice these acts of self-denial.

Self-denial covers a multitude of things. It is not only fasting from something to eat, or denying ourselves some desirable entertainment or recreation. It includes saying no, no, a thousand times no, to ourselves in such pleasurable little goodies as giving someone a piece of our mind; talking behind someone's back; wanting our own way too much; "letting George do it;" making excuses for our own faults and having intolerance for other people's faults, etc., etc. — so many etceteras. Most of these are little failings, but some are bigger and some can be down right deadly. St. Paul said, *"They who belong to Christ have crucified their flesh with its passions and desires."*

Does all this mean we have to sit with our eyes raised to heaven and our hands piously folded all the time? Of course not, but it does mean that we have to learn to keep those desires and their gratification in bounds. We have to learn to keep them within the curbstones of the roadway that Christ has walked.

It has our neighbor's needs in view, too. We should not forget our neighbor in the gratification of our own human and spiritual desires.

Self-denial is not without reward. It has its own built-in reward of freedom — freedom from runaway desires. We will find that there is a real satisfaction in that.

Remember, we are members of the "Order of Penance." We must make penance a part of our lives.

Now, from "Penance for the Future," a strong bulwark that it is against temptation and evil things that crop up from time to time, we come to "Penance for the Past."

Every "No" to God is a slap in His face. If we are truly sorry and ask him to forgive us He will, but we still owe Him a debt. An example of this is: if we break someone's window the owner may forgive us; but we still have to pay for a new window.

How do we pay our debt to God? We do it by "Penance for the Past."

"Penance for the Future," we have seen, strengthens us so we can resist sin. "Penance for the Past" is paying for sins actually committed — one prevents, the other heals.

"Penance for the Past" can simply be all our good actions offered to God.

Remember our Morning Offering — "All our prayers, works, joys and sufferings in reparation …" This is "Penance for the Past" right in our daily routine, our offering of little things to God. God likes little things. He does not expect us to climb a mountain, or swim a vast sea, or fast forty days and forty nights. Those things are for the one-of-a-kind type like Christ Himself, or for the one-in-a-million types, like St. Francis, St. Clare, the "Little Flower" and people like that. We are the little bitty ones that make up the rest of the millions.

If we do every little task and duty every day and bear every pain willingly for God's sake we would be doing perfect penance. It's as simple as that — and as hard as that.

This does not mean that we should not seek to alleviate our pains or to make our lives easier when we can. We are privileged to use the good things of life; to take aspirins, for instance; to make good use of work saving devices, or when we can, settle into a comfortable chair instead of choosing a hard bench. But, when something for instance cannot be mitigated then we should not waste the opportunity to "do penance." We have said this before: "Don't waste anything."

However, in our self-denials we should never abuse "brother body." Also, and this is important, we should keep our acts of self-denial quietly to ourselves — no looking for a pat on the back — self-denials lose much of their acceptability to God when we talk about them to others — bragging has its own reward.

This also applies to alms giving, which is another form of penance. Alms giving can include giving anything good — our time; our talents, such as they may be; personal help; money; clothing and other material things too numerous to mention. We can also offer our compassion; a smile; a word of encouragement and on and on. The quieter we are about these things the greater will be their value.

These penance's we have been talking about rise up and up to God in a real burst of glory when they become "Penance for Christ Crucified."

What is "Penance for Christ Crucified?" It is this: Willing to unite our penance's with Christ on His Cross. We are continuing Christ's work in the world today by willingly offering up our unavoidable sufferings and kicks in the teeth by life in union with His redemptive sufferings. We are then, right at this moment, sharing in His redemptive work. This is "Penance for Christ Crucified."

Someone has said, "A bed of pain has made many a saint, for when a person is flat on his back the only way to look is up." St. Francis suffered daily with Christ and wept many times over His sufferings.

Or, as Father Nimath said, "Suffering in itself is not good ... The pity is not that there is suffering in the world; but, that there is too much wasted suffering not united with Christ — too many crosses that never become crucifixes."

Or, still another quote of unknown origin: "It is much easier to let the cross hang on the wall than it is to carry it."

And now, with this, we can say we have scratched the surface of the subject of penance; but, we cannot leave it without some reference to the Sacrament of Penance.

We don't have to confess venial sins, but they should be avoided like the plague. Venial sins, carelessly accumulated, are spiritually debilitating. Just as Christ likes little good things, so does Lucifer chortle with glee over little bad things. The little bad things, when persisted in, have a way of dimming the lights so gradually that the darkening effect goes unnoticed until suddenly there is real danger of falling into some unseen pit.

St. Francis said, "I feel that I am the greatest sinner that ever existed." Well! If that holy man felt that way, the rest of us, at times, should feel a hot sulfuric breeze on the back of our necks.

But remember, our great saving virtues of faith and hope — faith and hope in God and in ourselves. Every time we make an *"Act of Contrition,"* a heartfelt one, it is an act of faith in the justice of God; an act of hope in the mercy of God and an act of our own worship and love for God.

We, who are of the "Order of Penance," should examine our consciences daily, and if in addition, we reverently make use of the Sacrament of Penance, we will find ourselves strengthened in purpose and increased in the holiness of the Holy Spirit. We say we are striving for perfection — all right then, we should soft-pedal our pride, our greed, our lust, our envy, our anger (in particular our revengeful anger) and our sloth or laziness in exerting ourselves to penance. We should show loud and clear what it means to be humble, patient, moderate, kind, meek, and poor in spirit.

"Learn of me," Jesus said, *"for I am meek and humble of heart and you shall find rest in your soul."*

That is really what all of us are longing for, to find peace in our soul. So, let us push steadfastly up our roadway, resolutely, doing penance as we go.

"... Poverty's twin — humility.
To have the one in its true spiritual
sense is to have the other ... "

Humility

St. Francis, in his beautifully simple and childlike way, looked upon the virtue of poverty as the quintessence of godliness. And equally important to this "little poor man" was the virtue he classed as poverty's twin — humility. To have the one in its true spiritual sense is to have the other — they walk hand in hand.

St. Francis said, "A man is what he is in the sight of God and nothing more," and in these words we have the twin virtues. To recognize that we are nothing without God is humility. To want nothing but God is poverty.

To be humble is to be aware of the basic truth of Christ's statement, *"He who abides in Me and I in him bears much fruit; for without Me you can do nothing,"*

We are nothing without God. We would not have life at all if God had not willed it, and without life, how could a nothing make a daily living, cook a meal, buy anything, sell anything, learn anything, laugh, talk and make progress of any kind? Some of these things we could accomplish with our backs turned to God. Many a so-called self-made man has reached the pinnacle of worldly success, with his back turned to God, but he would not have made it to kindergarten if God had not first put the breath of life in him. He would not have had a back to turn to God or a brain in his head; or even a head at all to use to achieve success — he would be a "nothing." And, that is just what he is even with his success, without God. King for a day he may be, but a nothing in space and time. To recognize these facts is to take the first step towards humility.

Christ, the Son of God, said, *"Of myself I can do nothing."* Mary matched this with her humility when she said, *"He has looked with favor on his lowly servant."*

Christ and Mary are models of humility and so is St. Joseph. Think of Bethlehem, and the stable with a poor man and woman and a baby lying on straw in an animal's manger. Who, other than Mary and Joseph, were the first living beings to lay eyes on the baby Son of God? Animals — an ox and an ass. No wonder the Jews could not, or would not recognize Him as the Savior and Messiah. They were expecting a glittering personage, a mighty ruler, a king bejeweled and resplendent in royal raiment. What did they get? A poor little baby born to a poor little family — but oh, what a baby. Humble He came and humble He went to His death. But in glory He rose and in glory forever He reigns, King of Kings and Lord of Lords! Out of humility came God, stooping down to us on earth to become one of us and out of humility we go to God rising up to become one of His very own.

Remember this: All by ourselves we are nothing, dingy specks of dust. But, let the rays of the sun filter through the dust and what do we see? A transmutation! Dust into gold. Touch the dirty little specks that we are with the rays of God's light and love and what do we see? Christ on the mountain, transfigured and we transmuted into something more precious than gold.

Children of the world, though they rise to the heights of success and pomp and power, remain drab little specks of dust, but the children of God, though they struggle along at the lowest level of the world's society, are princes and princesses in the royal household of God.

We must remember, and remind ourselves over and over that "my" house, "my" money, "my" talents", "my" brains," "my" this and "my" that are not mine at all; they belong to God, on loan to me while I live on earth, and those things are going to be left behind when I leave the earth. God is going to ask us a thing or two about them. What did we do with the 5, 10 or 100 talents He loaned to us to use? Did we develop them in the way He expected us to do, or did we bury them in the ground, to give them back to Him unused, soiled and corroded?

Now, to acknowledge our dependence on Him for everything is only one side of the coin of the virtue of humility. We also must be humble before our fellowman. We have said that each person is given certain gifts or talents and certain intelligence by God; some more, some less, but no matter how small, still most important. If an Einstein develops and uses his talents to the fullest extent he does not do one bit more than the poor little fellow who, just a shade above being a moron, develops and uses his poor little talents to the fullest degree. Both are equal in the sight of God. So, it ill behooves an intellectual giant to look down his nose on a mental dwarf.

An intellectual giant is so only because God endowed him with a superior brain. So too, the mental dwarf steps forth into life with the brain God gave him. The real worth is in the use to which each puts his gifts from God.

We should be humble, too, in looking upon the supposed faults of others. Are they really faults or just his different way of speaking, thinking, or doing? His fault, which in us might be a major sin, may not necessarily be a sin at all for him. We cannot judge his actions from our point of view which was gained in the cushion of our Christian homes or our background knowledge of right and wrong, and our gift of faith. Only God knows what lies behind another's actions. I am afraid that we tend to be much too lenient with ourselves, while leaping to harsh conclusions about the ways of others. Background, environment, home life, love, inherited traits, opportunities, and many other factors all play a part in what makes people tick.

No one knows the real truth of what makes someone do a certain thing except God, sometimes not even the person himself. We should not look down on anyone for his actions. Remember Christ's words, *"Let him who is without sin cast the first stone."* We need not approve of the acts of others, neither should we condemn. That is God's province.

St. Bonaventure said, "I must consider myself below others, not because I am certain that I am, but because I am more certain of my own unworthiness than I am of theirs." How few of us look so truly humbly into our own hearts and consciences.

One of the reasons St. Francis had such great influence on other people was because, though he was really such an exalted, good man, he walked always in the utmost humility. He was so very genuine.

The Friars Minor, or "Lesser Brothers," as he chose to call his first order, were humble people, low in the sight of the world, but who walked tall in the eyes of God. So also, should the lay Franciscan be — a little person who strives for God's eyes only; to walk humbly in a dignified manner in the eyes of man no matter what his position. This is exactly what it is to be a royal member of God's household; a nothing by worldly standards but a VIP by the standards of God.

This is our choice. But, even this, our choice, our desire to strive deliberately towards a closer union with God is not our own. It, too, is a gift of God, the gift of freedom of choice. We have our free wills only because God gave them to us as a gift.

Jesus said, *"Learn of me, for I am meek and humble of heart."* Sometimes it might strike us that a man who is meek and humble is a "milk toast." How absolutely opposed this is to the truth! It takes real strength and courage to hold back an angry retort or to resist a temptation. A meek man need not be a weak man. A weak man has no trouble at all in roaring out his anger, or yielding in to a temptation; it is easy to do and hard to hold back. A tantrum, the weapon of a child, has no place in the discipline of an adult.

What is the answer, then? How about the two "bears," "bear and forebear," the very adult, Christ-like weapons of a Christian man and woman.

Patience, meekness and humility — these are three little words. So are Christ, Mary and Joseph. The words are all cut out of the same cloth.

Father James E Sullivan, in his book, "My Meditations on the Gospel," says, "O Lord, teach me the serenity of patience and meekness. Help me to take people as I find them and life as it comes." The key word here is "serenity" — serenity of patience and meekness. These are not very desirable and very hard to attain, but how Christ-like they are. See how again and again we come back to Christ — patience, serenity, and meekness. These are all Christ synonyms.

Finally, in our consideration of the virtue of humility, we might think of Jesus, of His colossal humility and strength as He stood before the High Priest and Pilate and listened to the accusations and His sentence of death. Humble, but invincible, He stood there and "never said a murmuring word."

"When...one begins to go out
of one's way to help another,
to do things for him,
and in many different ways
to sacrifice one's self
for a person, then
we begin to have true love."

What is True Love

The great purpose of our lives is to love God and all the children of God. To understand this we go right back to the Gospels and through the words of Jesus Himself, when He answered the young lawyer's comment, *"what must I do to possess eternal life."*

Jesus answered him saying, *"you know the answer to that yourself. You tell me."* The lawyer then quoted scripture, *"Thou shalt love the Lord thy God with thy whole heart and thy neighbor as thyself."* And when the young man asked, *"who is my neighbor?"* Jesus told him the parable of the good Samaritan.

This brings up a good question. What is True Love?
First of all, it is a feeling towards someone that makes one feel like they want to be with that person, to talk with him, to do things together, and so on. That is, to a certain extent, a selfish aspect of love, a natural and human reaction, a reaching out towards other people and away from loneliness.

Now, when this feeling, this love for another person strengthens so that one starts thinking, not of one's own fulfillment, but a desire to wish good things for the other person then we take a step further in intensity. When the feeling is further strengthened to the point where one begins to go out of one's way to help another, to do things for him or her, and in many different ways to sacrifice one's self for this person, then we begin to have true love. This will bring an end to loneliness because a void in one's life has been filled.

From this human love, we progress to a greater love. How? By loving, not as we have just outlined, because we are attracted to someone and want to be with that person, but because we see a need in another person who may not necessarily be attractive at all; but in fact, may be an ugly, dirty, surly and an unpleasant character. One thing is certain, they are in need of something, maybe it is just a kind word, a smile, a recognition that they are a person who is, indeed, a person and not just a nothing. They are God's children, brother or sister like the leper Francis gave alms to and then kissed.

I believe that when we mention this incident of the leper in the life of St. Francis, we always think of Francis; his feelings, his revulsion, and his shuddering — forcing himself to kiss the leper.

But wait, and stop a minute. Think of the other side of this encounter. Think of the leper's feelings! Can you imagine how his heart must have leapt for joy; how his eyes must have widened with surprise at first, and then with joy when he experienced another human being, who, rather than shrinking away from him in fear and loathing him as was the usual pattern, smiled at him, and then, the wonder of wonders, actually threw his arms about him and embraced him?

That leper must have walked on air the rest of the day. His heart must have sung with wonder and joy in this Christ-happening — a joy he carried away with him into his lonely exile, and the aloneness with his horrible disease.

This is the great love, the love of Christ within us, sparking off a candle flame, a leaping joy in the life of another. This is Christ in us, joining in a warm, strong handclasp with the Christ in the other person. This is supernatural love.

No structure, that is the living temple of the Holy Spirit — the dwelling place of the great, boundless God and Spirit of Love, could possibly be really ugly or repulsive. We should seek the beauty of God's great love in that person, which beckons us to approach him in kindness and give him whatever we are able to give. Love such as this is very beautiful, very satisfying and very fulfilling — God then, is in our midst!

This is what it means to have "True Love" — to mold our existence around the living Christ. This is Franciscanism!

"It is a beautiful fact that our bodies are temples of God."

Chastity and the Body of Christ

I will not dwell long on the virtue of chastity, each one of us, whether married or single, knows what it means to be chaste; but, it is well for us to remember that Christ's human body and Mary's human body were exactly like ours and that they are our models of chastity.

"Do you not know," St. Paul said, *"that you are the temple of God and that the Spirit of God dwells in you?"*

When we take into our bodies the Sacred Host — the Body and Blood of Our Lord Jesus Christ — can we not think then of Christ, not only being part of our soul and our intellect, but our body as well — in short, a part of our whole humanity?

It is a beautiful fact that our bodies are temples of God. Believing this, we humbly keep in mind, that our bodies are really nothing more than animated clay, dust, and a handful of assorted chemicals, not worth very much of themselves. We cannot fail to grasp the sheer wonder of how these bodies of ours have been elevated to something more valuable than a pure gold chalice that holds the Blood of Christ. Our bodies are more precious than a gold tabernacle which houses the Sacred Host. Why? Because, kept chaste, they are a living home of God.

St. Paul said, *"If anyone destroys the temple, God will destroy him, for holy is the temple of God — you who receive His Most Precious Body are the temple of God."*

St. Paul also said, *"Do you not know that your members are the temple of the Holy Spirit, who is in you? You are not your own, for you have been bought at a great price."*

We human beings normally are not loners. We are a social lot. We like to mingle and laugh and enjoy ourselves with other human beings. It is pleasant to know that personal holiness does not mean we must forego the pleasures of life. What it does mean is that we should keep the presence of God in all our human activities at all times.

We will close with these remarks on chastity. It is impossible for the world to appreciate the idealism of chastity. There is so much confusion and trouble on the surface of life, so much weakness and rebellion in fallen human nature, that people find such idealism unbelievable. But, this idealism can be believable, and it is attainable. It should be the deliberate aim of every Christian man and woman.

*"The thing that really counts is
not what goes onto our bodies
but what comes out of our hearts."*

Medals and Scapulars

I'd like to reflect on the wearing of medals and scapulars and about having sacred statues and pictures in our homes. The reason I want to address this issue with you is that it bothers me the way some people are so hung up on these things, giving them an unreal importance and a power that was never intended (this is not to say that they are not important as a determent aginst the deceptions of Satan).

We were promised by the Blessed Virgin that if we are wearing the brown scapular at the time of our death we will be taken to heaven by our Lady shortly after our death. Then, we have the promise to Blessed Margaret Mary concerning making the nine first Fridays; and the promise from Fatima of our Lady regarding first Saturdays; and the promise about keeping a picture of the Sacred Heart in our homes, and so many other things like that.

Now, we could have 10 to 20 different medals, scapulars and such hanging around our necks at one time, and innumerable statues and pictures in our homes, and that is fine, I'm all for them, well at least one scapular or scapular medal which has Mary or the Sacred Heart. Our Franciscan medal or Tau Cross is top notch; it is our habit as Secular Franciscans. This is worn to express our promise to St. Francis and our affiliation with the Franciscan Order. What more do we need to wear?

A picture of the Sacred Heart is very good to have in our homes as well as a crucifix, and statues of Mary and other saints who influence our lives. But the thing that bothers me is the danger that we may place too much reliance on these "things" and these "promises" to get us from here to heaven.

One of the parables from St. Luke answers the question. (where else, but the Gospels do we get the answers to our questions). In this parable Jesus tells the story about the man who stored up great quantities of grain and then sat back with smug satisfaction and said, *"... You have all the good things you need for many years. Take life easy, eat, drink, and enjoy yourself"* But, God shook a finger right in his face and said, *"You fool, this very night you will have to give up your life; then who will get all these things you have kept for yourself? (Luke 12:19-20).*

So, there you are, in the Gospels we get it straight. None of these things, simply by the wearing or the using of them is going to get anyone to heaven.

The thing that really counts is not what goes onto our bodies but what comes out of our hearts (Gospel talk again) — what is given freely and cheerfully from inside ourselves, out to you Jesus, first with love, then out to our fellow man with love. This ends my problem with scapulars and medals, etc.

Notes

"Love suffering!
Are we out of our minds?"

Suffering

Our suffering can be a sacramental, something we can make holy by relating it to Christ's divine suffering. We also can make our suffering a quiet sacrifice by using it as an example to other people. There are so many examples of how to use suffering in Holy Scripture. Scripture shows us the way most pleasing to God. For example: Jesus, when He told the two brothers, James and John, *"You will indeed drink of the chalice that I shall drink."* Also, when He said, *"Deny yourself and take up your cross and follow me."*

Our suffering can be offered to God as a prayer. Too often, we are trying to get something from God rather than to give something. For a Franciscan, suffering has a special meaning. How do we react to suffering? Do we love suffering? Father Luke Ciampi, the author of "Watering the Seed," says, "Love suffering, are we out of our minds?" But, then he goes on to say, "The true Franciscan does not shut his eyes against suffering in this life. He accepts it as a dutiful reality he cannot avoid."

"The why-for-all of suffering is a refining process," He says, "the worthless things of the world are siphoned off." When life seems just simply too much, the Franciscan realizes that God tries us and sometimes pushes us to the absolute limit of our faith. He does so, not because he wants us to be miserable; but precisely, because he wants to stiffen our faith, to strengthen our hope and broaden our charity. "Do not hesitate," he says, "to use legitimate means to relieve suffering;" but, in doing so, acknowledge the hand of God sustaining you and helping you with His grace to bear it. It is in enduring and resigning oneself to the will of God that makes our suffering worthwhile. This attitude of resignation to God's will helps to make us spiritually healthy. The draining of the cup of suffering may taste bitter; but, its after-effect is sweeter than that of any nectar.

From another book, "Christ Among Us," we have this question: How can a good God allow suffering, particularly of the innocent? Some thought sickness came because of sin. Do you remember in John's Gospel, the episode of the blind man, where the disciples asked Jesus, *"who sinned to cause his affliction? Was it his own sin or those of his parents?"* And, Jesus answered flatly, *"It was neither."* I don't know whether you have noticed it or not; but, there is a tremendous amount of references to suffering in spiritual writings — biblical, Franciscan prayer books, writings of the saints, and many others. It is something that is our portion, as pilgrims, in this vale of tears.

Christ's Divine Suffering

Many eyes were fixed upon Him, many hands
reached out.
"Jesus, you are not alone; you've got us,"
they shout.

"Jesus, we adore you! This we'd
have you know,
That we will walk beside you, no matter
where you go.

Then He and all those people who were
dressed in shining white,
Marched resolutely forward straight
up to Calvary's height.

One cross, one man our Savior, on fire with
boundless love;
Bent by God Almighty from His heavenly
throne above.

It was sweat and blood so long ago,
there at Gethsemane;
He went from Bethlehem and Nazareth, to
The hill of Calvary.

This Man was sent from Heaven to endure
both pain and strife,
In order that mankind might share
His everlasting life.

Alleluia!

"Jesus, when you're ready,
I'm ready."

Sister Death

It seems not long ago when I was quite small I felt a feeling of being trapped when the days from September to the Christmas holidays just crawled. Then in time I took off like a runner at the Olympics, leaping over hurdles faster and faster while somewhere along the way I began to slow down slower and slower until here I am in the rarefied atmosphere of an octogenarian, with one foot in the grave and the other on a banana peel. It's not, I sighed, the first time I thought about Sister Death.

I think "ol' rocking chair's got me" and "the grass is greener on the other side of the fence." I think of that big Golden Gate ahead of me to which all of us, hopefully, are heading. I'm sure the grass is greener over there.

But really, it's nice and green right here and I have flowers and blue sky and white clouds, sometimes gray, and even black ones with lagged streaks of lightning tearing them apart. And, there is rolling thunder (the angels playing nine-pins my mother use to say). Its all so magnificent. But honest to goodness, I like it just fine on this side of the fence.

Somebody, I think it was Shakespeare, said: "Death, a necessary end, will come when it will come." And somebody, I think it was St. Paul, said, *"Death, where is thy sting?"* The Psalmist was encouraging when he said, *"The Lord is my shepherd, there is nothing I shall want. He will lead me in green pastures."* And, someone else said, *"He will wipe all the tears from your eyes."*

My grandmother used to send us girls books and one she sent was all in verse. One verse was about a child watching a pear tree and waiting for the pears to ripen. she said, "Little pear tree by the gate, how much longer must I wait?"

My rockin' chair is right over here. I shuffle slowly towards it, stepping very gingerly lest I disturb that banana skin under my foot, and I sit down and begin to rock.

"Jesus," I say, "when you're ready, I'm ready. Here I am outside your gate. It's up to you how long I wait. And I rock, rock, rock.

Have Sister Death open that Golden Gate and beckon me inside. Will you have my Blessed Mother, Mary walk beside me so I won't be afraid? Amen.

My Prayer to St. Francis

O great St. Francis, you are the shining knight --
the joyous singing troubadour of God;
who, down through the centuries
has strode like a Pied Piper of Jesus Christ
at the head of a great army of His children,
leading them on with your beckoning music,
straight to the mountain of God.

Help us, we pray, that your brothers and sisters
of your Secular Franciscan Order may
march joyously behind you as your little children;
and follow you on your road to the Heart of Jesus.

May we cry out as you did
when we feel His presence near us.
May our hearts reach out and up
to the great hope and expectation
of the fulfillment He has promised.

May we see the door of His great Heart
open to us, and may we, like trusting children,
go trooping inside into the foreverness of His love.

"My God and my All!" Amen.

I Asked Father Francis

I was walking to Church with St. Francis. The Angelus chimed in the morning air.

My thoughts were alive with questions. In my heart was a hymn and a prayer.

I saw that his eyes were upon me. On his lips was the faintest smile.

In the depths of his eyes there was something — was it wisdom or love without guile?

In a burst of affection I asked him, "Father Francis, how do you make amends

When you lose control of your temper and lash out at your friends?"

"Why," he said, "The answer is simple. The very first thing that you do

Is ask them for forgiveness and contrition will bring peace to you."

"What do you do," I asked him, "when the going is rough and you stumble and falter?"

He answered, "You'll find the going much smoother near Him at the foot of His altar."

I asked him, "What do you do when you have doubts and fears and thoughts are chaotic and wild?"

He smiled with eyes full of faith and said, "Go to your Mother in Heaven, my child."

I answered his smile and said, "What do you do, Father Francis, when you have to rise at the hour of five."

Hop out of bed, he said, take a deep breath and say, thanks be to God, I'm alive."

We could see the church now before us. Towards it we went on our way.

The air was cool and refreshing and I turned back to him to say ...

"What do, you do Father Francis, when your friends turn their backs on you?"

"Say, Father forgive them," he answered, "for they do not know what they do."

"Supposing," I said, "you ask for some bread and you receive a stone instead?"

He spread out his hands, what did He tell you? "Give us our daily bread."

I asked, "But what do you say of a woman who has been left abandoned and alone?"

He pondered a bit — "she should think of our Queen when they shut her Son in the tomb with a stone."

"What do you do," I cried fiercely, "when someone hits you with fist or rod?"

Back came his answer mildly. "You offer it up in union with Christ and say, Behold the Handmaid of God.!"

I asked him, "What do you do when someone whirls on you in an angry streak?"

Gently he said, "Why not shrug? Why not wink? Why not turn the other cheek?"

I faltered ... "You know, sometimes the way is dark and the path is foggy and dim."

His eyes took on a far-away look and said, "put all your trust in Him."

Sadly, then, I asked him, "what do you do when a loved one has died?"

I thought I saw a tear on his cheek, though his eyes were clear and wide.

He was quiet so long I persisted. "How do you bear the pain of such a loss?"

His voice was almost a whisper -- "You think of Him -- bleeding, bleeding to death on the cross."

At the door of the church I asked him, "How do you thank Him for the help He has given over the long, rough way we have trod?"

His voice became vibrant as music. "You cry, Glory and Praise and Thanksgiving — forever and ever, to God!"

Franciscan Mustard Seed

Francis sowed it in his garden,
His brothers tended it with care.
They fertilized it with their penance,
And watered it with tears and prayer.

It grew into the Gospel version —
A tree in which the birds could dwell.
It grew so big, its lofty branches
Sheltered the birds, and men as well.

Its seeds were caught up by breezes
And scattered thickly here and there.
They grew into ten thousand others
That spread their branches everywhere.

Now in the day, eight centuries later,
We reap the fruit sown ages past;
By Francis and his holy brothers,
And now it is our turn at last.

To plant some seeds in other gardens;
To nurture them with work and care.
To fertilize them with our penance,
And water them with love and prayer.

Our hope is to grow in Gospel's version;
Great, with roots set firmly in the sod;
To fling more seeds down through the ages
And draw a million souls to God.

Ruth Vogel

Notes

Pax et Bonum
Peace and Good

www.ingramcontent.com/pod-product-compliance
Lightning Source LLC
Chambersburg PA
CBHW020502030426
42337CB00011B/195